THE WAY I'M
WIRED

discovering who GOD made ME to be

Katie Brazelton

FOREWORD BY DOUG FIELDS

The Way I'm Wired
Discovering Who God Made ME To Be

Copyright © 2011 Katie Brazelton

group.com
simplyyouthministry.com

Credits
Author: Katie Brazelton
Executive Developer: Nadim Najm
Chief Creative Officer: Joani Schultz
Editor: Rob Cunningham
Cover Art and Production: Jeff Storm, Veronica Lucas, and Riley Hall
Back Cover Author Picture (Katie Brazelton): Images by Dwayne
Production Manager: DeAnne Lear

Unless otherwise indicated, all Scripture quotations are taken from the *Holy Bible*, New Living Translation, copyright © 1996, 2004, 2007. Used by permission of Tyndale House Publishers, Inc., Carol Stream, Illinois 60188. All rights reserved.

Scripture quotations marked The Message are taken from *The Message*. Copyright © 1993, 1994, 1995, 1996, 2000, 2001, 2002. Used by permission of NavPress Publishing Group.

ISBN 978-0-7644-4704-4

10 9 8 7 6   20 19 18 17 16

Printed in the United States of America.

CONTENTS

PART II: NEW TESTAMENT

FOREWORD
DOUG FIELDS

You don't know who I am, and you probably don't care, but I've been around ministry to teenagers for a long time. I'm passionate about lots of things—including Jesus, my family, friends, mountain biking, Chick-fil-A®, Twizzlers®, and Diet Coke®.

Seeing teenagers discover their life purpose is another one of my greatest passions, and that's why I'm glad you have this book in your hands! I've had the privilege as a youth pastor of helping thousands of teenagers walk the path you're about to walk, so I can write with confidence that God has incredible things in store for you as you work through this book.

I'm so proud of the work my good friend Katie Brazelton has done with this devotional—written just for you. She's dug through all 66 books of the Bible—yup, even the ones with peculiar names that you've probably never read—and has uncovered some of the most meaningful verses about the adventure of discovering and fulfilling God's best for your life. You are in for a wild ride!

I'd encourage you to do three things as you read this book:

- **Write.** Katie has crafted a highly interactive book with lots of space to write your thoughts and answers to specific questions, so keep a pen or pencil with you every time you grab this book. In addition to writing in the provided spaces, break the "rules" and write along the margins, circle verses and phrases that grab your attention, jot down your questions with a big red marker…basically, do whatever you feel like doing as you engage with this material. Make it your own.

- **Ask.** As you're going through this devotional, you may read a verse or something Katie wrote that brings up questions. Awesome! Sit down with your parents, your youth pastor, your small group leader, or some other trusted friend (who may know a little more than you) and ask your questions over some beverage or food (making sure they buy, of course).

- **Pray.** OK, I probably should have made this my first piece of advice! Begin your adventure with prayer. Maybe you feel pressure to discover God's purpose as if it's some hidden level on a video game or a hidden bargain at the mall. Guess what? You don't have to figure it out on your own. Invite God to reveal your life's purpose and mission, and to help you understand the powerful mission God created *just for you*.

Some people talk about teenagers being the church of tomorrow. I don't believe that! I believe just the opposite, I'm convinced that teenagers who follow Jesus are actually the church of today. You don't have to wait until you're older to do something big for God; you can do it now—and understanding your unique mission is a key step in accomplishing big things for God.

My prayer is that you'll enjoy the journey that follows this page!

Doug Fields

INTRODUCTION

"The rain and snow come down from the heavens and stay on the ground to water the earth. They cause the grain to grow, producing seed for the farmer and bread for the hungry. It is the same with my word. I send it out, and it always produces fruit. It will accomplish all I want it to, and it will prosper everywhere I send it" (Isaiah 55:10-11).

Do you find yourself asking any of these questions about your life purpose?

- Why was I born?

- Where do I fit in this world?

- Will my dreams ever come true?

- Is this all there is to life?

- What on earth am I here for?

It's important to have your questions answered from a biblical perspective, before you even jump in to the life purpose devotionals for each of the 66 books of the Bible! So, here we go:

- You were born to bring glory to God.

- You fit perfectly into God's perfect plan to redeem the world.

- God has dreams for you to pursue that are beyond your wildest imagination.

- An abundant, joyful, purpose-filled life awaits you—the life you're meant to live.

- You're on earth to complete God's three purposes for your life. It's important to do this in true *trifecta* fashion—with all three purposes working together in perfect harmony to unleash God's best for you and for the people you're sent to serve!

Biblical Purpose Trifecta: 1-2-3

1. Universal Purpose: Love God by belonging to Christ.

Your purpose is to love God by choosing to be transformed into a new person in the image of Christ. This happens by reading God's Word and allowing the Holy Spirit to teach you to surrender to Jesus Christ as Lord. This means that, with the help of your church family (including prayer partners, accountability partners, and mentors), you're committed to a life of holiness, integrity, right motives, peace, and worshipping your Creator—and helping others to do the same.

Scriptural Basis

- *Jesus replied, "'You must love the Lord your God with all your heart, all your soul, and all your mind.' This is the first and greatest commandment" (Matthew 22:37-38).*

- *Don't copy the behavior and customs of this world, but let God transform you into a new person by changing the way you think. Then you will learn to know God's will for you, which is good and pleasing and perfect (Romans 12:2).*

- *Jesus told him, "I am the way, the truth, and the life. No one can come to the Father except through me" (John 14:6).*

2. Universal Purpose: Love God by loving others.

Your purpose is to love God by doing today—with love—what matters today in the responsibilities, daily tasks, and major roles God has assigned you. This includes honoring your Maker by serving with Christ-like love in all your life domains: personal, family, relationships, school, job, ministry, and community. This means that you trust in the Lord for strength and power to fulfill your commitments and meet the challenges that drive your day at home, school, work, and church, and in your neighborhood and ministry setting, and on your mission field.

Scriptural Basis

- Jesus added, *"A second [commandment] is equally important: 'Love your neighbor as yourself' " (Matthew 22:39).*

- *This is the message you have heard from the beginning: We should love one another (1 John 3:11).*

- *No one has ever seen God. But if we love each other, God lives in us, and his love is brought to full expression in us (1 John 4:12).*

3. Unique Purpose: Glorify God by fulfilling your "This I Must Do" Dream.

Your purpose is to glorify God by doing the "One Big Thing" God commissioned you—and you alone—to do to help build the kingdom. This unique, individual, significant purpose directs you to pursue your God-designed life mission with pure joy and to deliver your God-inspired life message to those you're eager to serve. This purpose is God's personalized gift to you, and it's a dream that reflects your passionate ache, your Divine Urge, your heart's desire, and the fascination that was planted in your soul before you were even born. It's what drives your life—what you feel you must do. It's what you're called to do—what you feel you *can't not do*! But you must decide if you'll actually take on this huge commitment to make this eternal contribution that's impossible to do without God's help.

Scriptural Basis

- *"I [Jesus] brought glory to you here on earth by completing the work you gave me to do" (John 17:4).*

- *"In the same way that you gave me [Jesus] a mission in the world, I give them a mission in the world" (John 17:18 The Message).*

- *Take delight in the Lord, and he will give you your heart's desires (Psalm 37:4).*

It's natural to have a strange reaction to the hard-to-comprehend idea that you have a fascinating, custom-made purpose assigned by God. For example, you may feel...

- I'm not worthy enough, smart enough, or holy enough to shoulder the responsibility of a personalized, impassioned life mission that God will reveal.

- The dream I'm sensing must be of my own making, because of prideful and selfish desires I have.

- God, you're a taskmaster, and I know you'll assign me something too difficult and too unappealing. Frankly, I don't really want to know what my mission is, because I don't want to end up as an overseas missionary.

- I don't have the right motives, spiritual gifts, or character traits to complete the task—and, anyway, I'm comfortable in the current roles God delegated to me.

The truth is that none of us is good enough to measure up to the task of doing something magnificent for the Lord—and we all have tons of doubts, concerns, and fears. Thank heavens that it's only by the grace and power of God that we'll be able to answer the long-term call on our life, so we can't boast that it's of our own doing.

This book is jam-packed with a collection of Scriptures dedicated to the topic of God's universal purposes and unique plan for your life—an ingenious plan that's based on how you've been wired and equipped! Your reading and reflection time is designed to help you discover who you were made to be, including how you've been intricately outfitted and readied to fulfill God's plan for your life.

We rest on the promise that God's Word will bear fruit in you (Isaiah 55:10-11). So, fasten your seat belt and expect life-changing, personal discoveries about *what on earth you're here for*!

Fulfill Your God-Given, "This I Must Do" Dream

God is famous for planting *must-do* assignments in people's hearts. Consider these life-changing ones:

- **Noah,** build an ark before the great flood. (Genesis 6:13-21)

- **Abram,** go to the land I'll show you—without knowing any specifics. (Genesis 12:1-3)

- **Sarah,** you'll be the mother of nations at the age of 90. (Genesis 17:15-16)

- **Moses,** go to Pharaoh and demand the release of my people. (Exodus 3:10, 20)

- **Gideon,** go with the strength you have and rescue Israel from the Midianites. (Judges 6:12-16)

- **Samuel,** anoint David king (in spite of ensuing turmoil). (1 Samuel 16:12-13)

- **John the Baptist,** prepare the way for me. (Luke 1:13-17)

- **Mary,** you're a virgin but you'll give birth to a Son who will reign with an everlasting kingdom. (Luke 1:28-38)

- **Peter,** feed my lambs. (John 21:15-17)

- **Paul,** proclaim the good news to the Gentiles. (Galatians 1:13-16)

The list goes on and on—moments when God commissions ordinary people to do extraordinary things that take a lifetime to see to final completion or when God calls ordinary people to complete an impossible task that defines and shapes the rest of their lives. Why would you be an exception to that pattern of the ordinary person being used to do the extraordinary? God is glorified when you're stretched beyond your personal ability to complete an impossible task.

May God's Word bless you as you ponder ideas, journal your answers, and conclude that you want to live more decisively, energetically, and faithfully for your Maker. May God's perfectly crafted plan for your life jump off the pages. May you begin, now, to discover and fulfill the perfect-for-you life purpose that was put in your heart eons ago. And may you enjoy the adventure!

My prayer is that God will reveal your bold, exhilarating life mission that will bring you pure joy at just the thought of it. I also offer this heartfelt blessing based on 2 Timothy 2:21 as you travel this journey to purpose:

I pray that you will be an instrument for noble purposes, made holy, useful to the Master and prepared to do any good work.

Blessings,

Katie Brazelton

HOW TO GET THE MOST OUT OF THIS DEVOTIONAL

"For I [Jesus] have come down from heaven to do the will of God who sent me, not to do my own will" (John 6:38).

Not your ordinary devotional book

This devotional is loaded with 200 Scripture passages from all 66 books of the Bible about the incredible destiny God designed especially for you, including your unique life purpose. Feel free to skip around, or read straight through from Genesis to Revelation. The power of God's Word will challenge you to consider your most engaging, broad-reach life purpose, like you might never have done before. I urge you to breathe in the verses and prayers, not just read them. Immerse yourself in the scenes with the men and women of the Bible. Allow God to speak to you as if you're sitting together sharing a meal.

Q: How long will this devotional book take me to read?

A: It depends how you choose to approach the reading, reflecting, and journaling of your answers. The book is filled with...

- **25 Digging Deeper** stories about men and women of the Bible. Each entry has Background Information, Reflection Questions, and a brief prayer.

- **103 On-the-Go** and **Sitting Awhile** passages with Life Purpose Applications (Apps) and questions for times when you want to see what a certain book of the Bible has to say about your purpose in life. Some days, you might choose to enjoy a Scripture for a moment; other days, you'll want to sit longer to soak in more of God's Word.

- **44 BONUS ROUND** references about other biblical people of purpose. Choosing to look up these stories will shed even more light on God's distinct and specific recommendations for your life.

- **28 other supporting passages** that relate directly to God's plan for your life.

Some days you'll sail through one or two stories and/or read two or three related passages. Other days, God may lead you to set up camp on a certain page. So, plan on enjoying the journey for approximately 35 days—give or take a few days.

Q: How difficult are the questions?

A: The questions are down-to-earth and designed to draw out personal applications to your life, but you'll be digging deep inside, for sure, to uncover truths about yourself and God's plan for you. Here's a sample of two questions you might encounter: *In what ways has God been faithful to you in the past? What does this tell you about God's faithful love that will work out all the future details of your life?*

Q: What am I supposed to do in the MULLING THINGS OVER area?

A: When you see this area of blank space, that's your signal to draw a picture, write a song, journal your thoughts, or tape in a photo or other keepsake related to your life purpose. Or you can do a *brain dump* list of the things causing your mind to wander—as you pray for God to reveal your boldest life purpose.

PART 1

OLD TESTAMENT

GENESIS

Abraham's Purpose: To be the father of a great nation.

Background: Notice that Abram, whose name hadn't been changed yet to Abraham, is being sent! To reveal your life purpose, God may call you out of a role or situation—and/or call you to a new beginning. Both legs of the journey are equally important tests of obedience for you: to be willing to leave the old and begin the new.

The Call of Abram. *¹The Lord had said to Abram, "Leave your native country, your relatives, and your father's family, and go to the land that I will show you. ²I will make you into a great nation. I will bless you and make you famous, and you will be a blessing to others. ³I will bless those who bless you and curse those who treat you with contempt. All the families on earth will be blessed through you" (Genesis 12:1-3).*

Reflection Questions:

1. When and why has God called you out of a particular situation? For example: to walk away from a friend who's a bad influence; leave a ministry role you love, so you can learn different skills; get out of

your comfort zone and give a speech; repent from a sin to get a fresh start with Jesus; get away from a negative group of friends to develop healthier relationships.

When:

Why:

2. If you dared to daydream about *God calling you* to a unique, exciting life mission that would bless a large group of people for the Lord, what details about the when, where, and to whom might your dream include?

When:

Where:

To Whom:

Prayer: God, make me willing to leave behind whatever you command and to go whenever, wherever, and to whomever you send me, even if you don't reveal all the details.

GENESIS BONUS ROUND: Check out these other *call* stories:

- 6:13-21—**Noah** was called to build an ark before the great flood.

- 17:15-16—**Sarah**, who'd been barren all her life, was called to be the mother of nations at the age of 90.

- 28:10-15—**Jacob** heard God's will for him in a dream.

- 37:5-11—**Joseph** learned in a dream that he'd rule over others.

EXODUS

Moses' Purpose: To lead God's people out of Egypt.

Background: God got Moses' attention by appearing to him in a blazing fire from the middle of a bush. Moses stared in amazement because the bush was engulfed in flames, but it didn't burn up. That day, God called Moses to a mighty task: to free the Israelites from Egyptian captivity.

The Call of Moses at the Burning Bush. *[10]"Now go, for I [God] am sending you [Moses] to Pharaoh. You must lead my people Israel out of Egypt. ...[20]So I will raise my hand and strike the Egyptians, performing all kinds of miracles among them. Then at last he will let you go. [21]And I will cause the Egyptians to look favorably on you. They will give you gifts when you go so you will not leave empty-handed" (Exodus 3:10, 20-21).*

Reflection Questions:

1. What message have you received from God, even if it didn't involve a burning bush? For example, God showed up to tell you: I am God—and I love you, forgive you, miss you, caution you, am calling you, grieve with you, will protect you, or am proud of you.

2. Is God calling you to a mighty task? For example: free slaves who are captive to sin by praying for them; work with the homeless; write and sing songs that honor God; step up to a leadership role; do a spiritual fast from gossip, music, or shopping; launch a ministry. Why do you think that?

Prayer: God, give me the courage not to "pull a Moses" by echoing his words: *"Lord, please! Send anyone else" (Exodus 4:13)*. Give me the grace to accept and enjoy my assignment.

EXODUS BONUS ROUND: Check out God's purpose for these people:

- 2:1-10—**Moses' mother and his sister Miriam** hid baby Moses, even though it meant risking death. (See Hebrews 11:23 about the faith and courage of Moses' parents when *they saw that God had given them an unusual child*.)

- 4:27—**Aaron** was called to *"go out into the wilderness to meet Moses."* Little did he know what tough assignment awaited him!

- 9:16—**Pharaoh**, a stubborn ruler, was even usable by God, who said of the obstinate man, *"I have spared you for a purpose—to show you my power and to spread my fame throughout the earth."*

LEVITICUS

Holiness. *"For I am the Lord your God. You must consecrate yourselves and be holy, because I am holy" (Leviticus 11:44).*

- **Life Purpose Application (App): Your primary purpose in life is to bring glory to God by being holy.** Being holy means that you're consecrated or dedicated to God—that you're willing to be set apart to do God's will. Why isn't holiness optional? In what way can you dedicate yourself now to a life of holiness to prepare for a potentially daunting and humanly impossible assignment?

LEVITICUS BONUS ROUND: Check out God's call of Aaron to the priesthood:

- 8:12—**Aaron** was anointed with oil by Moses, who consecrated him as a priest.

Mid-air Adjustment. While seated, make clockwise circles with your right foot. At the same time, draw the number "6" in the air with your right hand. Your foot will change direction—that's a scientific fact. Another tricky thing to do is to simultaneously rotate the index fingers of both hands clockwise. Go faster and faster, and pretty soon your two fingers will be going in opposite directions! Wild, huh? Likewise, even if your life is going in one direction right now—let's say, away from holiness—God can easily make a mid-air adjustment for you, even though that new direction may seem impossible to you right now. If you need to ask for God's help, just ask for it.

MULLING THINGS OVER

(Draw a picture, write a song, journal your thoughts, or tape in a photo or other keepsake related to your life purpose. Or you can do a *brain dump* list of the things causing your mind to wander—as you pray for God to reveal your boldest life purpose.)

NUMBERS

Following the Fiery Cloud. *¹⁷Whenever the cloud lifted from over the sacred tent, the people of Israel would break camp and follow it. And wherever the cloud settled, the people of Israel would set up camp. ¹⁸In this way, they traveled and camped at the Lord's command wherever he told them to go. Then they remained in their camp as long as the cloud stayed over the Tabernacle (Numbers 9:17-18).*

- **Life Purpose App: Break camp and set up camp at the Lord's command.** When have you traveled or camped at the Lord's command—moved on or stayed put—in hobbies, spiritual habits, education, training, a club/organization, personal growth, or volunteer work? Any brand-new marching orders that will allow you to practice obedience for your unique life mission?

Fearing the Giants. *⁷They [Joshua and Caleb] said to all the people of Israel, "The land we traveled through and explored is a wonderful land! ⁸And if the*

Lord is pleased with us, he will bring us safely into that land and give it to us. It is a rich land flowing with milk and honey. ⁹Do not rebel against the Lord, and don't be afraid of the people of the land. They are only helpless prey to us! They have no protection, but the Lord is with us! Don't be afraid of them!"

¹⁰But the whole community began to talk about stoning Joshua and Caleb. Then the glorious presence of the Lord appeared to all the Israelites at the Tabernacle. ¹¹And the Lord said to Moses, "How long will these people treat me with contempt? Will they never believe me, even after all the miraculous signs I have done among them?" (Numbers 14:7-11).

- **Life Purpose App: Don't be afraid.** God protects. If you'd been one of the 12 spies exploring the land of Canaan, would you have been more like the 10 who came back fearful of the "giants" in the land or more like Joshua and Caleb, who believed in God's protection in spite of the dangers? Why?

Commissioning of Joshua. *¹⁸The Lord replied, "Take Joshua son of Nun, who has the Spirit in him, and lay your hands on him. ¹⁹Present him to Eleazar the priest before the whole community, and publicly commission him to lead the people. ²⁰Transfer some of your authority to him so the whole community of Israel will obey him" (Numbers 27:18-20).*

- **Life Purpose App: Accept the authority bestowed on you.** In your wildest imagination, if God commissioned or blessed you to have an entire community of people follow you, what would you like to do for the Lord with all that authority and support?

God expects of us the one thing that glorifies Him—and that is to remain absolutely confident in Him, remembering what He has said beforehand, and sure that His purposes will be fulfilled.

~ Oswald Chambers, Scottish Protestant minister, 1874-1917

DEUTERONOMY

Israel's Rebellion Against the Lord. *42 "But the Lord told me [Moses] to tell you, 'Do not attack, for I am not with you. If you go ahead on your own, you will be crushed by your enemies.' 43 This is what I told you, but you would not listen. Instead, you again rebelled against the Lord's command and arrogantly went into the hill country to fight. 44 But the Amorites who lived there came out against you like a swarm of bees. They chased and battered you all the way from Seir to Hormah. 45 Then you returned and wept before the Lord, but he refused to listen"* (Deuteronomy 1:42-45).

- **Life Purpose App: Obey God's instructions or suffer the consequences.** When have you disobeyed, disrespected, or disagreed with an earthly authority figure or God? What consequences did you suffer? Examples could include pain, loss, punishment, embarrassment, shame, abandonment, restitution, or repayment. How might rebellion against God's commands create consequences for the purpose God has for your life?

A Call to Love and Obedience. *"And now, Israel, what does the Lord your God require of you? He requires only that you fear the Lord your God, and live in a way that pleases him, and love him and serve him with all your heart and soul"* (Deuteronomy 10:12).

- **Life Purpose App: Fear, please, love, and serve God with all your heart and soul.** What will your cooperation with God (fearing, loving, pleasing, and serving God) say to people in your life about your unfolding vision from God?

A Call to Obey the Lord's Commands. *[17]"You have declared today that the Lord is your God. And you have promised to walk in his ways, and to obey his decrees, commands, and regulations, and to do everything he tells you. [18]The Lord has declared today that you are his people, his own special treasure, just as he promised, and that you must obey all his commands. [19]And if you do, he will set you high above all the other nations he has made. Then you will receive praise, honor, and renown. You will be a nation that is holy to the Lord your God, just as he promised"* (Deuteronomy 26:17-19).

- **Life Purpose App: Obeying God opens the door to great rewards.** God promised the nation of Israel some incredible blessings in return for obedience. Do you think God promises to bless you and your future, too, if you walk in his ways and do everything he tells you? How would you like your future to be blessed?

Titanic. It cost $7 million to build the Titanic and $200 million to make a movie about it. If you eagerly obeyed God's titanic, colossal, immense, gigantic call on your life, what might you be able to build, make, invent, or establish for God with $207 million? (Yes, your passion will create a blockbuster buzz!)

MULLING THINGS OVER

(Draw a picture, write a song, journal your thoughts, or tape in a photo or other keepsake related to your life purpose. Or you can do a *brain dump* list of the things causing your mind to wander—as you pray for God to reveal your boldest life purpose.)

JOSHUA

The Lord's Charge to Joshua: To march around Jericho with his fighting men and priests for seven days, until the walls collapsed and they could take the city.

Background: This book opens just after Moses died; Deuteronomy 34:10 speaks his final praises: *There has never been another prophet in Israel like Moses, whom the Lord knew face to face.* Imagine being Joshua (Moses' assistant), trying to fill your boss' shoes. Wouldn't you feel a little intimidated and afraid? No wonder God had to remind Joshua three times in the first nine verses of this book to be strong and courageous. In fact, Joshua 1:7 says: *strong and very courageous.*

In fact, how'd you like to have been Joshua when God said, *"The time has come for you to lead these people, the Israelites, across the Jordan River into the land I am giving them" (Joshua 1:2)*? A little worried and panicked? No wonder God gave Joshua detailed instructions about how to capture Jericho.

The Fall of Jericho. *¹Now the gates of Jericho were tightly shut because the people were afraid of the Israelites. No one was allowed to go out or in. ²But the Lord said to Joshua, "I have given you Jericho, its king, and all its strong warriors. ³You and your fighting men should march around the town once a day for six days. ⁴Seven priests will walk ahead of the Ark, each carrying a ram's*

13

horn. On the seventh day you are to march around the town seven times, with the priests blowing the horns. ⁵When you hear the priests give one long blast on the rams' horns, have all the people shout as loud as they can. Then the walls of the town will collapse, and the people can charge straight into the town." ...

²⁰When the people heard the sound of the rams' horns, they shouted as loud as they could. Suddenly, the walls of Jericho collapsed, and the Israelites charged straight into the town and captured it (Joshua 6:1-5, 20).

Reflection Questions:

1. What Jericho wall (such as a lack of energy, health, time, experience, credibility, focus, partnerships) is standing between you and God's best life for you? Will you march around that wall courageously, believing that God has claimed victory over it?

2. The town of Jericho was the first stop for the Israelites in the Promised Land. What has God revealed to you so far about your Promised Land—your divine destination and God's perfect plan for your life?

Prayer: God, your mighty power is evident in the way you chose to destroy Jericho. Show me that same unmatched power, as you move me into my Promised Land.

JUDGES

God's Command to Barak: To call out 10,000 warriors to fight, knowing God was marching ahead of them.

Background: Deborah, a prophetess and the only known female judge of Israel, summoned Barak, who was her countryman, to tell him that God was ready to deliver their enemies of 20 years into his hands. He ended up refusing to go without her, so she went with him and the victory was hers.

Get Ready! [6][Deborah said to Barak,] *"This is what the Lord, the God of Israel, commands you: Call out 10,000 warriors from the tribes of Naphtali and Zebulun at Mount Tabor.* [7]*... There I will give you victory over him [Sisera]."* [8]*Barak told her, "I will go, but only if you go with me."* [9]*"Very well," she replied, "I will go with you. But you will receive no honor in this venture, for the Lord's victory over Sisera will be at the hands of a woman." So Deborah went with Barak to Kedesh. ...* [14]*Then Deborah said to Barak, "Get ready! This is the day the Lord will give you victory over Sisera, for the Lord is marching ahead of you"* (Judges 4:6-9, 14).

Reflection Questions:

1. When have you bravely done what God commanded you to do? Maybe you've served, attended, spoken, written, asked, forgiven, voted, boycotted, studied, resisted, fled, affirmed, or surrendered. How confident did you feel, knowing your action was an act of obedience?

2. If you knew for sure that the Lord was marching ahead of you to give you victory, what might you attempt to do for God?

Prayer: God, when you tell me to "Get ready!" because you'll be marching ahead of me to give me victory, send the extreme courage I need to obey you.

JUDGES BONUS ROUND: Check out these call stories:

- 6:12-16—**Gideon**, a judge and warrior, was called into action by God, who told him: *"Go with the strength you have, and rescue Israel from the Midianites. I am sending you!"* (v. 14)

- 13:1-5—**Samson** was chosen by God as a Nazirite from birth and called to *"begin to rescue Israel from the Philistines."* (v. 5)

Since I had given myself to Jesus in order to please Him and comfort Him, I must not oblige Him to do my will instead of His.

—Saint Thérèse of Lisieux, French nun, 1873-1897

RUTH

God's Plan for Ruth, a Widow: To be an ancestor of David and Jesus—with her second husband Boaz (after the death of her first husband).

Background: Ruth was a faithful, loving, and enterprising woman who felt convicted to stay with her mother-in-law Naomi, even though both their husbands had died. Little did Ruth know that God was guiding her step-by-step along a path that would allow her to become the great-grandmother of King David and an ancestor of Jesus. (The first chapter of Matthew provides the full chronology, if you enjoy reading lists of names!) She didn't know the ultimate result of her obedience, but she willingly followed God's purpose.

Ruth Is Loyal and Kind. *[16]But Ruth replied, "Don't ask me to leave you and turn back. Wherever you go, I will go; wherever you live, I will live. Your people will be my people, and your God will be my God. [17]Wherever you die, I will die, and there I will be buried. May the Lord punish me severely if I allow anything but death to separate us!" [18]When Naomi saw that Ruth was determined to go with her, she said nothing more (Ruth 1:16-18)*

Reflection Questions:

1. In what way(s) are you like Ruth—faithful, loving, or enterprising/ innovative? How could God use character traits like those to help you fulfill a humanly impossible life mission?

2. Which unlovely character trait from your life would you want eliminated? Examples might include pride, impatience, greed, aggression, jealousy, bitterness, judgmental attitude, passivity, intolerance, undisciplined mouth, ungratefulness, or wastefulness. Why did you choose that trait?

Prayer: God, help me act daily in a loyal, kind-hearted, and resourceful way, as if I were a great-, great-, great-(X lots more greats) great-grandparent of Jesus.

Superman and His Wife. In his offscreen life, actor Christopher Reeve (who portrayed Superman in four movies) loved sports, whether that was sailing, scuba diving, skiing, aviation, windsurfing, cycling, gliding, parasailing, mountain climbing, baseball, tennis, or horseback riding. In 1995, Reeve was thrown headfirst from his horse during a jumping competition, and he sustained a cervical spinal injury that paralyzed him from the neck down. He died in 2004, but not before he inspired people worldwide to live life to the fullest. His wife Dana, an actress, singer, and remarkable woman who also inspired countless to "take up a cause to save lives," was diagnosed with cancer less than a year after her husband's death. She died in 2006. In what way would you like to be an inspiration to others by the way you live your life?

1 SAMUEL

Samuel's Mission: To anoint David.

Background: Samuel had the distinction of anointing Saul as the first king of Israel and David as the second. He often advised them and knew full well their strengths and sins. Samuel saw firsthand that God sometimes uses sinners to accomplish what needs to be done for kingdom growth and that sin unleashes harsh consequences.

Samuel Anoints David as King. *¹²So Jesse sent for him. He was dark and handsome, with beautiful eyes. And the Lord said, "This is the one; anoint him." ¹³So as David stood there among his brothers, Samuel took the flask of olive oil he had brought and anointed David with the oil. And the Spirit of the Lord came powerfully upon David from that day on. Then Samuel returned to Ramah (1 Samuel 16:12-13).*

Reflection Questions:

1. Who in your circle of friends or role models has accepted God's call and commissioning? Why do you think that?

2. Even though the prophet Samuel isn't standing over you right now you with a flask of oil, do you believe that God wants you for kingdom service? Why or why not? (No fair playing the *I'm a sinner* card here! We're all sinners.)

Prayer: God, thank you for your willingness to trust me with a lifetime assignment. Help me respond faithfully to your call on my life.

1 SAMUEL BONUS ROUND: Check out these stories about extraordinary purpose:

- 1:1-28—**Hannah** poured her heart out in prayer, saying that if God blessed her with a son, she'd dedicate him to the Lord's service. Later, Hannah conceived Samuel and took him to the temple to live.

- 3:1-18—**Samuel**, Hannah's son who lived and served in the temple, heard God calling him as a young boy. He replied, "*Speak, your servant is listening*" (v. 10). Then Samuel delivered the message God had given him.

- 17:1-58—**David**, a teenage shepherd, went out to meet the giant Goliath. He chose not to wear a helmet and coat of armor, but he went equipped with a slingshot, five smooth stones, and God's power. Not only did David slay Goliath that day, but he eventually became the king of Israel.

- 25:14-44—**Abigail** became known as the first female public relations official because she made a "pitch" to David, the future leader of Israel, as to why he shouldn't kill her foolish husband, Nabal. She said, "*Don't let this be a blemish on your record*" (v. 31)—and she showered David with a lavish gift of provisions for his army. She had incredible courage and wisdom in the face of imminent danger—and she later became David's wife after Nabal had a stroke and died.

2 SAMUEL

David's Purposeful Decision: To confess his guilt, accept the consequences of his sins, and answer God's call on his life.

Background: King David, a giant-slayer, powerful warrior, cunning diplomat, and talented musician/poet, brought the tribes of Israel together as a united nation. But he also committed a long list of sins, including lust, adultery, and murder. Yet God never stopped loving him. After David's confession of guilt and time of severe consequences, God moved forward with the plan to send the Savior through David's family line by making David an ancestor of Jesus' earthly father Joseph.

David Confesses His Guilt. *Then David confessed to Nathan, "I have sinned against the Lord." Nathan replied, "Yes, but the Lord has forgiven you, and you won't die for this sin."*

Reflection Questions:

1. Why do you think God allows us imperfect people to have significant life assignments?

2. If you could recommend a consequence for one of your sins, what would it be? Do you think that's tougher or easier than God would be on you?

Prayer: God, I come humbly before you to confess all my sins, especially

_____.

I accept the consequences for what I've done, because I no longer want anything to stand in the way of honoring you and following the spectacular, strategic plan you have for my life.

Marley & Me. The 2005 New York Times bestselling book *Marley & Me: Life and Love With the World's Worst Dog* is a true story by journalist John Grogan. Marley, a yellow Labrador Retriever, was obedience-challenged and high-strung. He was a demolition derby but a friend like none other. When Marley died, Grogan wrote a memorial tribute in his newspaper column that got more reader response than any other column he'd ever written, and this inspired him to write the full story of Marley's life. Little did the author know that his book would be made into a 2008 film that would require 18 different dogs to capture the spirit of the rambunctious Marley or that the movie would set a record for the largest Christmas Day box office sales ever! If a movie were to be made about your life, would it depict an obedience-challenged person—a demolition derby in motion? Or would it reveal a life defined by obedience to God?

1 KINGS

Digging deeper into... 1 Kings 8:17-21

Solomon's Mission: To build God's Temple in Jerusalem.

Background: Solomon, the third king of Israel, never learned moderation. He had a lust for power, prestige, and women. In spite of this, God made him the richest and wisest man on earth and placed a distinct call on his life. Unlike his father, King David, Solomon was a man of peace. God rewarded that core value and destined him to build the ancient Jerusalem Temple, a magnificent house of worship that was the center of life for the Jews.

Solomon Praises the Lord. *[17] Then Solomon said, "My father, David, wanted to build this Temple to honor the name of the Lord, the God of Israel. [18] But the Lord told him, 'You wanted to build the Temple to honor my name. Your intention is good, [19] but you are not the one to do it. One of your own sons will build the Temple to honor me.' [20] And now the Lord has fulfilled the promise he made, for I have become king in my father's place, and I now sit on the throne of Israel, just as the Lord promised. I have built this Temple to honor the name of the Lord, the God of Israel. [21] And I have prepared a place there for the Ark, which contains the covenant that the Lord made with our ancestors when he brought them out of Egypt" (1 Kings 8:17-21).*

Reflection Questions:

1. What big, great, difficult, or challenging work would you most want to do for God?

2. God used Solomon powerfully, even though Solomon would later make choices that displeased God, including worshipping idols and false gods. How many "mini-gods" do you worship? That would include anything that occupies the top spot that belongs to God, such as popularity, prestige, fame, fortune, possessions, food, painkillers, a celebrity, or a hero.

Prayer: God, I'll do whatever you've planned for me to do—big or small, elaborate or simple, now or later. I ask specifically for your wisdom and provision—and also your protection from sin.

1 KINGS BONUS ROUND: Check out these stories about God's gifts of wisdom, wealth, an action plan, and anointing for service:

- 3:1-28—**Solomon** asked for wisdom, and God granted his request—and so much more.

- 19:9-18—**Elijah** heard God speak in a gentle whisper and then received an action plan.

- 19:19-21—**Elisha** was anointed by the prophet Elijah and became his apprentice.

2 KINGS

Elisha and the Woman From Shunem. *⁸One day Elisha went to the town of Shunem. A wealthy woman lived there, and she urged him to come to her home for a meal. After that, whenever he passed that way, he would stop there for something to eat. ⁹She said to her husband, "I am sure this man who stops in from time to time is a holy man of God. ¹⁰Let's build a small room for him on the roof and furnish it with a bed, a table, a chair, and a lamp. Then he will have a place to stay whenever he comes by"* (2 Kings 4:8-10).

- **Life Purpose App: Your purpose is to show God's love to others through acts of kindness.** You may not be able to add a room to your house, like the woman in this story, but how can you perform deliberate and random acts of kindness? Why are thoughtfulness and helpfulness important characteristics for anyone living out God's unique plan?

MULLING THINGS OVER

(Draw a picture, write a song, journal your thoughts, or tape in a photo or other keepsake related to your life purpose. Or you can do a *brain dump* list of the things causing your mind to wander—as you pray for God to reveal your boldest life purpose.)

Only a life lived for others is worthwhile.

—Albert Einstein

1 CHRONICLES

The Purpose of David's Questions/Prayers: To seek God's specific advice about what to do next.

Background: First Chronicles provides a historical chronicling and recording of the family tree of God's people from Adam to King David. But here's a little insight about how David relied on God, just after he'd been anointed Israel's second king.

David Conquers the Philistines. *⁹The Philistines arrived and made a raid in the valley of Rephaim. ¹⁰So David asked God, "Should I go out to fight the Philistines? Will you hand them over to me?" The Lord replied, "Yes, go ahead. I will hand them over to you." ¹¹So David and his troops went up to Baal-perazim and defeated the Philistines there. "God did it!" David exclaimed. "He used me to burst through my enemies like a raging flood!" So they named that place Baal-perazim (which means "the Lord who bursts through"). ¹²The Philistines had abandoned their gods there, so David gave orders to burn them.*

¹³But after a while the Philistines returned and raided the valley again. ¹⁴And once again David asked God what to do. "Do not attack them straight on," God replied. "Instead, circle around behind and attack them near the poplar trees. ¹⁵When you hear a sound like marching feet in the tops of the poplar trees, go out and attack! That will be the signal that God is moving ahead of you to strike down the Philistine army." [16]*So David did what God commanded, and they struck down the Philistine army all the way from Gibeon to Gezer.* [17]*So David's fame spread everywhere, and the Lord caused all the nations to fear David (1 Chronicles 14:9-17).*

Reflection Questions:

1. When have you recently sought God's advice about what step to take or which path to choose? What was the result of following God's way—or the consequence of not following his way?

2. If you knew that God was willing to give you excellent advice as you worked on your boldest life purpose—and he *is* willing—what would that do for your confidence level?

Prayer: God, I want nothing more than to do your will, so I need to hear from you on a regular basis about my next steps. Teach me to ask you for specific instructions along the way, like David did.

The study of God's Word, for the purpose of discovering God's will, is the secret discipline which has formed the greatest characters.

—James Waddel Alexander, American Presbyterian minister, 1804-1859

2 CHRONICLES

Check out the friendship between Hezekiah and God:

¹Hezekiah was twenty-five years old when he became the king of Judah, and he reigned in Jerusalem twenty-nine years. ...²He did what was pleasing in the Lord's sight, just as his ancestor David had done (2 Chronicles 29:1-2).

"But now I [Hezekiah] will make a covenant with the Lord, the God of Israel, so that his fierce anger will turn away from us" (2 Chronicles 29:10).

At the same time, God's hand was on the people in the land of Judah, giving them all one heart to obey the orders of the king and his officials, who were following the word of the Lord (2 Chronicles 30:12).

And the Lord listened to Hezekiah's prayer and healed the people (2 Chronicles 30:20).

Then the priests and Levites stood and blessed the people, and God heard their prayer from his holy dwelling in heaven (2 Chronicles 30:27).

In all that he did in the service of the Temple of God and in his efforts to follow God's laws and commands, Hezekiah sought his God wholeheartedly. As a result, he was very successful (2 Chronicles 31:21).

²⁰Then King Hezekiah and the prophet Isaiah son of Amoz cried out in prayer to God in heaven. ²¹And the Lord sent an angel who destroyed the Assyrian army with all its commanders and officers. So Sennacherib was forced to return home in disgrace to his own land (2 Chronicles 32:20-21).

²⁴About that time Hezekiah became deathly ill. He prayed to the Lord, who healed him and gave him a miraculous sign. ²⁵But Hezekiah did not respond appropriately to the kindness shown him, and he became proud. So the Lord's anger came against him and against Judah and Jerusalem. ²⁶Then Hezekiah humbled himself and repented of his pride, as did the people of Jerusalem. So the Lord's anger did not fall on them during Hezekiah's lifetime (2 Chronicles 32:24-26).

- **Life Purpose App for These Eight Passages: God partners with those seeking to do their life's work.**

SUMMARY QUESTIONS FOR 2 CHRONICLES: These eight passages create a great outline of the type of relationship God wants to have with you:

- Do what's pleasing in God's sight.

- God's fierce anger will turn away.

- God's hand will be on you.

- God will hear you and heal you.

- You'll be successful.

- God will watch over you.

- You'll receive miraculous signs.

What does this covenant or agreement suggest to you about your next step toward God's passionate call on your life? Will you take that step?

How Google® Got Its Name!

The term "googol" is a mathematical term for 10^{100}, which is a useful number when comparing unimaginably large numbers with infinity. The word was introduced formally in 1940 by American mathematician Edward Kasner, whose 9-year-old nephew reportedly invented it when asked to think up a very big number![1]

In 1995, Google's founding partners, Larry Page and Sergey Brin, met as students at Stanford University, and soon came up with the name Google—a play on the word googol—for their search engine. The use of the term reflected their mission to organize a seemingly infinite amount of information on the web. As this highly promising project developed, the two students managed to attract investors, and Google Inc., opened for business in a friend's garage on September 7, 1998, in Menlo Park, California.[2]

If you knew you'd have unprecedented success, even more so than Larry Page and Sergey Brin, and if you truly understood that God partners with those seeking to do kingdom-building work, what would you attempt as your life mission—even if you started in a friend's garage?

MULLING THINGS OVER

(Draw a picture, write a song, journal your thoughts, or tape in a photo or other keepsake related to your life purpose. Or you can do a *brain dump* list of the things causing your mind to wander—as you pray for God to reveal your boldest life purpose.)

EZRA

Sitting awhile with Ezra...

As the Israelites returned from exile, they rebuilt Jerusalem and the Temple. What do the following verses say about God's help for Israel?

But because their God was watching over them, the leaders of the Jews were not prevented from building until a report was sent to Darius and he returned his decision (Ezra 5:5).

There was great joy throughout the land because the Lord had caused the king of Assyria to be favorable to them, so that he helped them to rebuild the Temple of God, the God of Israel (Ezra 6:22).

[Many years later, Ezra] came up to Jerusalem from Babylon, and the king gave him everything he asked for, because the gracious hand of the Lord his God was on him (Ezra 7:6).

I [Ezra] felt encouraged because the gracious hand of the Lord my God was on me (Ezra 7:28).

Since the gracious hand of our God was on us, they sent us a man named Sherebiah, along with eighteen of his sons and brothers (Ezra 8:18).

And the gracious hand of our God protected us and saved us from enemies and bandits along the way (Ezra 8:31).

- **Life Purpose App for These Six Passages: God's gracious hand is on your "This I Must Do" mission.**

SUMMARY QUESTIONS FOR EZRA: The Jews' enemies, who tried to block their success at every turn, were no match for God! The book of Ezra is clear that as you tackle the enormous tasks assigned you, God will…

- watch over you

- create favor for you

- provide resources for you

- give you encouragement

- send helpers to assist you

- protect you

- save you from your enemies

When have you felt the gracious hand of God on your life, and what does that teach you about your future? What does this list suggest to you about your next step toward God's exhilarating call on your life? Will you take that step?

NEHEMIAH

The Burden God Put on Nehemiah's Heart: To repair the wall of Jerusalem that had been torn down and the gates that had been destroyed by fire.

Background: In Chapter 2, Nehemiah talks about the specific, inspired plan God had put in his heart to repair Jerusalem's wall and gates—with the help of those returning from Babylonian captivity. He had covered the entire construction project in prayer and fasting, right from the moment he first heard about the problem. Miraculously, he was granted permission from the king of Persia, his boss at the time, to go to Jerusalem. Then he stayed focused until the rebuilding was completed, even when his enemies taunted his workers.

Nehemiah Felt Called to Jerusalem. *²I asked them [my brothers from Judah] about the Jews who had returned there from captivity and about how things were going in Jerusalem. ³They said to me, "Things are not going well for those who returned to the province of Judah. They are in great trouble and disgrace. The wall of Jerusalem has been torn down, and the gates have been destroyed by fire." ⁴When I heard this, I sat down and wept. In fact, for days I mourned, fasted, and prayed to the God of heaven.*

5Then I said, "O Lord, God of heaven, the great and awesome God who keeps his covenant of unfailing love with those who love him and obey his commands, 6listen to my prayer! Look down and see me praying night and day for your people Israel. I confess that we have sinned against you. Yes, even my own family and I have sinned! 7We have sinned terribly by not obeying the commands, decrees, and regulations that you gave us through your servant Moses.

8Please remember what you told your servant Moses: 'If you are unfaithful to me, I will scatter you among the nations. 9But if you return to me and obey my commands and live by them, then even if you are exiled to the ends of the earth, I will bring you back to the place I have chosen for my name to be honored.' 10The people you rescued by your great power and strong hand are your servants. 11O Lord, please hear my prayer! Listen to the prayers of those of us who delight in honoring you. Please grant me success today by making the king favorable to me. Put it into his heart to be kind to me" (Nehemiah 1:2-11).

Reflection Questions:

1. Nehemiah wept, mourned, fasted, prayed, confessed, recounted God's promise, begged that God would hear his prayer, and asked God specifically for success. Which of those elements are "your style" when you talk to God? Why might it be helpful to add a new habit to your prayer life from Nehemiah's list or another habit like singing, meditation, silence, memorizing and reciting Scripture, or spiritual journaling?

2. What big burden, lifetime longing, or passionate purpose has God laid on your heart to pursue? What investigative step can you take in that direction?

Prayer: God, if Nehemiah could be so bold in his prayers to you—and you answered him favorably—then allow me to pray that you grant me success by making this burden on my heart work out favorably: _____

_____

ESTHER

Esther's Purpose: To save the Jews from destruction.

Background: Esther needed to ask her husband, the king, to save the Jews (her people) from being killed. Her Uncle Mordecai had sent her this message: *"If you keep quiet at a time like this, deliverance and relief for the Jews will arise from some other place, but you and your relatives will die. Who knows if perhaps you were made queen for just such a time as this?" (Esther 4:14).* Esther made up her mind to risk violating the rules of the king's court by going before him without being invited. Before she went in, though, she was wise enough to call for a three-day fast and prayer service for all the Jews in the city.

Esther Was Made for Such a Time As This. Esther sent this reply to her uncle: *"Go and gather together all the Jews of Susa and fast for me. Do not eat or drink for three days, night or day. My maids and I will do the same. And then, though it is against the law, I will go in to see the king. If I must die, I must die" (Esther 4:16).*

Reflection Questions:

1. If you had God's permission and resources to save somebody (one person, a few people, or a large, international people-group) from something, whom would you save from what—and why?

2. What risk is God asking you to take that will help you explore a richly fulfilling purpose that is larger than you and impossible to do on your own?

   On this risk scale, where would you rank the action and why?

   1 = It's simple   5= This is tough   10= It's a life-altering risk

Prayer: God, give me the courage to be a risk-taker regarding the steps I feel you want me to take toward a life of significance.

Esther, a Woman of Few Words. According to ABC News (Ashley Phillips, July 5, 2007) reporting on a study from the University of Arizona, it's no longer believed that women speak three times as many words as men! The study concluded that males and females both use on average 16,000 words per day. Esther sure knew how to cut to the chase with just a few words when she gave her famous speech in Esther 4:16 that ended with *"If I must die, I must die."* What few words or sentences would sum up your willingness to commit to a cause to which God called you?

JOB

Job's Purpose-Filled Trials: To love and trust God, whether blessings abound or not.

Background: Satan proposed to God that Job was a good and righteous man simply because of all the protection and blessings he received from God. So, Satan was allowed to take Job's wealth, children, and physical health in an effort to tempt him to abandon his faith. True, Job does get a bit rattled during the trials and inappropriately challenges God's wisdom, but he also said things like this: *"But as for me, I know that my Redeemer lives, and he will stand upon the earth at last" (Job 19:25).* The end of the story is that Job was restored to an even better condition than his former state, and he lived another 140 years.

In God's Hand is Everyone's Life. *10When Job prayed for his friends, the Lord restored his fortunes. In fact, the Lord gave him twice as much as before! 11Then all his brothers, sisters, and former friends came and feasted with him in his home. And they consoled him and comforted him because of all the trials the Lord had brought against him. And each of them brought him a gift of money and a gold ring.*

¹²So the Lord blessed Job in the second half of his life even more than in the beginning. For now he had 14,000 sheep, 6,000 camels, 1,000 teams of oxen, and 1,000 female donkeys. ¹³He also gave Job seven more sons and three more daughters. ¹⁴He named his first daughter Jemimah, the second Keziah, and the third Keren-happuch. ¹⁵In all the land no women were as lovely as the daughters of Job. And their father put them into his will along with their brothers. ¹⁶Job lived 140 years after that, living to see four generations of his children and grandchildren. ¹⁷Then he died, an old man who had lived a long, full life (Job 42:10-17).

Reflection Questions:

1. Have you experienced a crisis, emergency, trauma, disaster, or long-term trial during which you put your hope in God? In what way were you able to share the reason for your hope with others?

2. How would you feel about having a life purpose that involved passing a difficult "life test," like Job's, that would make you a role model for generations to come?

Prayer: God, you give and you take away. Regardless of whether you bless me or not, help me love you always for who you are—not for what you can do for me.

PSALMS

David's Cry for Mercy. *I cry out to God Most High, to God who will fulfill his purpose for me (Psalm 57:2).*

- **Life Purpose App: Cry out to God Most High, who will fulfill your purpose.** Against all odds, God protected David from King Saul, until it was time to fulfill David's blessed purpose of becoming Israel's second king. In what way do you know, hope, or pray that God will show up for you to fulfill your blessed purpose?

The Lord's Plan. *The Lord will work out his plans for my life—for your faithful love, O Lord, endures forever. Don't abandon me, for you made me (Psalm 138:8).*

- **Life Purpose App: Rest assured that your loving God will work out the plans for your life.** In what way has God been faithful to you in the past? What does this tell you about God's ability to bless all the future details of your life?

Book of Life. *You saw me before I was born. Every day of my life was recorded in your book. Every moment was laid out before a single day had passed (Psalm 139:16).*

- **Life Purpose App: Ask God to reveal every purpose for your life that was laid out before you were born.** If you were God (not gonna happen, but just pretend for a moment!), what would you design for you to do with your life? In what way might some part of that impossible-sounding dream be God speaking directly to you right now?

OTHER GREAT PURPOSE VERSES IN THE PSALMS:

- **2:1**—*Why do they waste their time with futile plans?*

- **33:11**—*But the Lord's plans stand firm forever; his intentions can never be shaken.*

- **40:5**—*O Lord my God, you have performed many wonders for us. Your plans for us are too numerous to list.*

- **73:24**—*You guide me with your counsel, leading me to a glorious destiny.*

The Book of Psalms Is Centered on God. Here's a little bit of Bible trivia for you. Psalm 118 is the middle chapter of the Bible. It has 594 chapters before it and 594 chapters after it. If you add the two sides together, you get 1,188. What's the verse at the very center of the Bible? Psalm 118:8: *It is better to take refuge in the Lord than to trust in people.* That's pretty cool, isn't it? Centering your life on God means getting centered on God's Word. Two additional fun factoids: Psalm 117 (just prior to 118) is the shortest chapter of the Bible, and Psalm 119 (just after) is the longest chapter of the Bible.

PROVERBS

Seek and Trust. *Seek his [God's] will in all you do, and he will show you which path to take (Proverbs 3:6).*

- **Life Purpose App: God will show you which path to take for all you do—your role is to seek and obey.**

The Right Answer. *We can make our own plans, but the Lord gives the right answer (Proverbs 16:1).*

- **Life Purpose App: God will give you the right answer regarding what plans are best for you.**

The Lord's Purpose. *You can make many plans, but the Lord's purpose will prevail (Proverbs 19:21).*

- **Life Purpose App: God's purpose will prevail.**

Even the Wicked. *God made everything with a place and purpose; even the wicked are included—but for judgment (Proverbs 16:4 The Message).*

- **Life Purpose App: God has an end purpose for everything, even for the wicked: a day of disaster.**

SUMMARY QUESTIONS FOR PROVERBS: In what way is it comforting to know that you don't have to rely on your own path, answers, life purpose, or understanding? What do these four practical applications suggest as a next step for you toward God's unique plan? Will you take that step?

- God will show you the correct path.

- God will give you the right answer.

- God's purpose will prevail.

- God has an end purpose for everything, even for the wicked: a day of disaster.

OTHER GREAT PURPOSE VERSES IN PROVERBS:

- **16:9**—*We can make our plans, but the Lord determines our steps.*

- **16:33 (The Message)**—*Make your motions and cast your votes, but God has the final say.*

- **21:30**—*No human wisdom or understanding or plan can stand against the Lord.*

No Need to Stress About Your Life Plan! Stress can cause or complicate all kinds of health issues: heart disease, chronic fatigue, anxiety attacks, mood swings, depression, sleep problems, high blood pressure, eating disorders, chronic pain. It's incredible that the one thing you don't have to stress about is designing a perfect plan for your life. God has already created a unique and magnificent plan that will prevail.

ECCLESIASTES

The Master's Plan. *Yet God has made everything beautiful for its own time. He has planted eternity in the human heart, but even so, people cannot see the whole scope of God's work from beginning to end (Ecclesiastes 3:11).*

- **Life Purpose App: God created a master plan from beginning to end.** You can rest in the fact that God has a major, strategic plan in place. How does knowing that affect the personal agenda you've set for your life?

God's Finished Plan. *And I know that whatever God does is final. Nothing can be added to it or taken from it. God's purpose is that people should fear him (Ecclesiastes 3:14).*

- **Life Purpose App: Your purpose is to fear God.** God created an eternal plan that remains constant for all time. Let this truth cause a deep sense of reverence in you for your Maker. In fact it's meant to stir up a holy fear, which is a combination of respect, wonder, and awe for the Master Planner and a deep desire to please and love the One who created you. All this leads us to an attitude of wanting to do what God wants. It's about God's will, not our wishes. In what way does holy fear prompt you to want to leave the legacy you've been intricately wired to leave?

Christian Duty. *¹³That's the whole story. Here now is my final conclusion: Fear God and obey his commands, for this is everyone's duty. ¹⁴God will judge us for everything we do, including every secret thing, whether good or bad (Ecclesiastes 12:13-14).*

- **Life Purpose App: Your duty/purpose is to fear and obey God.** Solomon, whose wisdom was second only to Jesus, searched and searched for the truth about living a life filled with significance. His conclusion was that our life purpose is simple: to fear and obey God. By this, Solomon is recommending that you be filled with a wholesome dread of displeasing your loving Creator but not with a terror that causes you to shrink in God's presence. How have fear and obedience been tied together for you in a negative way? In what way does Solomon's combo of *fear and obey* make sense to you? In the future, will your holy fear be more like (a) humility in the face of God's greatness or (b) the anxiety of being disciplined by a cruel judge?

God alone satisfies.

—Thomas à Kempis, medieval Catholic monk

SONG OF SONGS

Groom declares: *You have captured my heart, my treasure, my bride. You hold it hostage with one glance of your eyes, with a single jewel of your necklace. [10] Your love delights me, my treasure, my bride. Your love is better than wine, your perfume more fragrant than spices (Song of Songs 4:9-10).*

Bride declares: *I am my lover's, and he claims me as his own (Song of Songs 7:10).*

- **Life Purpose App: God's purpose for physical intimacy is to express love in marriage (and to have children).** Many scholars see this book as an allegory about God and the people of Israel. The chapters seem to reveal a picture of God's adoring devotion. Any adultery (loving something or someone more than God) is out of the question because it damages that relationship. Other scholars believe that this Old Testament book is simply showing the pure, passionate, and sensual love between a bride and groom. Are your sexual choices harming the relationship God wants to have with you and the exceptional purpose God has for your life?

MULLING THINGS OVER

(Draw a picture, write a song, journal your thoughts, or tape in a photo or other keepsake related to your life purpose. Or you can do a *brain dump* list of the things causing your mind to wander—as you pray for God to reveal your boldest life purpose.)

SUGGESTION FOR SUCCESS

Selecting a Scripture as your life verse can be extremely helpful in focusing you on true success! To find a verse that fits the theme of your unique life mission, begin with prayer. Pray often that God will choose to reveal it to you. Waiting for God's revelation, though, can feel like a matter of "Which comes first—the chicken or the egg?" For example...

- **Chicken comes first:** God gives you a life verse that births your life mission!

- **Egg comes first:** God gives you a life mission that births your life verse!

Whichever ends up working best for you, let God do the revealing and let God be glorified by the tandem confirmation that the verse gives the mission and the mission gives the verse.

Bottom line: Memorizing and reflecting often on your life verse will help you move toward true success and enjoy that success when you get there! Keep your heart open for your life verse to be revealed. Does any Scripture jump out at you now?

ISAIAH

The Best Response to God's Call: To answer, like Isaiah, "Here I am. Send me."

Background: This book is called *The Book of Salvation* because the name Isaiah means the Lord is salvation[3]—and Isaiah foretold the coming of the Messiah, urging the people to repent from their sins. As a prophet, he was a deeply spiritual man who was particularly passionate about reaching the nation of Judah.

- **A Message for Rebellious Judah.** *¹It was in the year King Uzziah died that I saw the Lord. He was sitting on a lofty throne, and the train of his robe filled the Temple. ²Attending him were mighty seraphim, each having six wings. With two wings they covered their faces, with two they covered their feet, and with two they flew. ³They were calling out to each other, "Holy, holy, holy is the Lord of Heaven's Armies! The whole earth is filled with his glory!" ⁴Their voices shook the Temple to its foundations, and the entire building was filled with smoke.*

  ⁵Then I said, "It's all over! I am doomed, for I am a sinful man. I have filthy lips, and I live among a people with filthy lips. Yet I have seen the King, the Lord of Heaven's Armies." ⁶Then one of the seraphim flew to me with a burning coal he had taken from the altar with a pair of tongs. ⁷He touched my lips with it and said, "See, this coal has touched your lips. Now your guilt is removed, and your sins are forgiven." ⁸Then I heard the Lord asking, "Whom should I send as a messenger to this people? Who will go for us?" I said, "Here I am. Send me." ⁹And he said, "Yes, go." (Isaiah 6:1-9).

Reflection Questions:

1. God seems to have doubly blessed Isaiah's passionate desire to be a useful messenger, possibly because Isaiah was so eager to serve even though he felt inadequate. Isaiah had such an incredible speaking and writing ministry that he has even been nicknamed the *Prince of Prophets* and *Shakespeare of the Bible*. How could God use your passion and giftedness to reach people—even if you, too, feel inadequate?

2. Strong tradition suggests that Isaiah died a martyr's death under the reign of King Manasseh by being placed in the hollow of a tree trunk and sawed in two. What are you called to do with your life, shy of dying a martyr's death, so that Christ-followers are encouraged by your Isaiah-like passion for the Lord?

Prayer: God, you are holy, holy, holy—the Lord of Heaven's Armies! Thank you for removing my guilt and forgiving my sins. Help me to pray boldly, like Isaiah, "Here I am. Send me."

PURPOSE VERSES IN ISAIAH:

- **25:1**—*O Lord, I will honor and praise your name, for you are my God. You do such wonderful things! You planned them long ago, and now you have accomplished them.*

- **30:1**—*"What sorrow awaits my rebellious children," says the Lord. "You make plans that are contrary to mine. You make alliances not directed by my Spirit, thus piling up your sins."*

- **45:13**—*"I will raise up Cyrus to fulfill my righteous purpose, and I will guide his actions. He will restore my city and free my captive people— without seeking a reward! I, the Lord of Heaven's Armies, have spoken!"*

- **64:4**—*For since the world began, no ear has heard, and no eye has seen a God like you, who works for those who wait for him!*

MULLING THINGS OVER

(Draw a picture, write a song, journal your thoughts, or tape in a photo or other keepsake related to your life purpose. Or you can do a *brain dump* list of the things causing your mind to wander—as you pray for God to reveal your boldest life purpose.)

JEREMIAH

A Teenager's Best Response to God's Call: To obey when the Lord says: *"Don't say, 'I'm too young,' for you must go wherever I send you and say whatever I tell you"* (Jeremiah 1:7).

Background: Scholars believe that God called Jeremiah, the son of a priest, to be a prophet when he was between 14 and 21 years old. Jeremiah's audience was God's chosen people, the rebellious Judah. His message was to urge the people to submit to their deserved punishment and surrender to Babylon. For this, Jeremiah was considered a traitor and was viciously persecuted.

Jeremiah's Call and First Vision. *⁴The Lord gave me this message: ⁵"I knew you before I formed you in your mother's womb. Before you were born I set you apart and appointed you as my prophet to the nations." ⁶"O Sovereign Lord," I said, "I can't speak for you! I'm too young!"*

⁷The Lord replied, "Don't say, 'I'm too young,' for you must go wherever I send you and say whatever I tell you. ⁸And don't be afraid of the people, for I will be with you and will protect you. I, the Lord, have spoken!" ⁹Then the Lord reached out and touched my mouth and said, "Look, I have put my words in your mouth! ¹⁰Today I appoint you to stand up against nations and kingdoms. Some you must uproot and tear down, destroy and overthrow. Others you must build up and plant."

[11] Then the Lord said to me, "Look, Jeremiah! What do you see?" And I replied, "I see a branch from an almond tree." [12] And the Lord said, "That's right, and it means that I am watching, and I will certainly carry out all my plans." …[17] "Get up and prepare for action. Go out and tell them everything I tell you to say. Do not be afraid of them, or I will make you look foolish in front of them" (Jeremiah 1:4-12, 17).

God's role in young Jeremiah's mission:

- *I knew you before I formed you*
- *Before you were born I set you apart*
- *I appointed you as my prophet*
- *I'll be with you and will protect you*
- *I've put my words in your mouth*
- *Today I appoint you*
- *I'm watching*
- *I'll certainly carry out all my plans*

Young Jeremiah's role:

- *You must go wherever I send you*
- *Say whatever I tell you*
- *Get up and prepare for action*
- *Go out*
- *Tell them everything I tell you to say*
- *Don't be afraid of them*

Reflection Questions:

1. In what way have you felt resistant to God's call on your life because you see yourself as too young, too unworthy, too unprepared, too uneducated, too ill equipped, too unattractive, too poor, or some other "too"?

2. If you heard God telling you today to "go wherever I send you and say whatever I tell you," where would you hope you'd be sent (your own hometown, locally, nationally, abroad), and what words do you hope God would put in your mouth as your life message?

Prayer: God, thank you that I'm sufficient in your sight—and that you called me and equipped me. Make me willing to go *at whatever age* to *wherever* you choose to send me with *whatever* message you assign me to deliver.

MULLING THINGS OVER
(Draw a picture, write a song, journal your thoughts, or tape in a photo or other keepsake related to your life purpose. Or you can do a *brain dump* list of the things causing your mind to wander—as you pray for God to reveal your boldest life purpose.)

JEREMIAH

The Lord's Plan. *¹⁰This is what the Lord says: "You will be in Babylon for seventy years. But then I will come and do for you all the good things I have promised, and I will bring you home again. ¹¹For I know the plans I have for you," says the Lord. "They are plans for good and not for disaster, to give you a future and a hope. ¹²In those days when you pray, I will listen. ¹³If you look for me wholeheartedly, you will find me. ¹⁴I will be found by you," says the Lord. "I will end your captivity and restore your fortunes. I will gather you out of the nations where I sent you and will bring you home again to your own land"* (Jeremiah 29:10-14).

- **Life Purpose App: God knows the end of your story, which is to bring you home again with a good future.** The prophet Jeremiah had sent a letter (Jeremiah 29:1-23) to some of the exiles that Nebuchadnezzar had taken from Jerusalem to captivity in Babylon (modern-day Iraq). Verse 11 is his most famous good news message, because it referred to the end of their captivity. But the bad news of his letter was that those people of Judah would have to brace themselves for 70 years in exile! So, Jeremiah needed to make sure the captives heard that their gracious God still loved them and had a plan for them, even though the wait for relief was going to be long. How long do you think will you have to wait for God's good plan to launch itself in your life? Should you start praying now that it's not going to be 70 years? Regardless of how long it takes, will you wait patiently for the Lord?

ANOTHER GREAT PURPOSE PASSAGE IN JEREMIAH:

- **32:38-40**—*[38]"They will be my people, and I will be their God. [39]And I will give them one heart and one purpose: to worship me forever, for their own good and for the good of all their descendants. [40]And I will make an everlasting covenant with them: I will never stop doing good for them."*

CAMELS

Here are some facts you may not know about camels:

- They can go up to two weeks without water and up to a month without food.

- They can survive at least a 25 percent body weight loss due to sweating.

- They can swim.

- They have extra-long eyelashes that help keep sand out of their eyes.

- They can close their nostrils to keep sand out of their noses.

- They have a split upper lip that moves independently, so they can get near the ground to eat.

- They have wide, padded feet that grip well and prevent them from sinking into the sand.

- They have a thick wool coat that reflects sunlight.

- They have one or two mounds that store fatty tissue (not water, as is commonly thought) from which they can draw energy when food is hard to find.[4]

Some have even said that camels were the inspiration for the rumbling growl that helped create Chewbacca's voice in the Star Wars movies!

If God poured this much creativity, magnificence, and adaptability into camels, how much more has been poured into you to prepare you for your life mission? In God's eyes, is there such a thing as too young, too unworthy, too unprepared, too uneducated, too ill equipped, too unattractive, too poor, or some other "too"?

LAMENTATIONS

Hope in God's Faithfulness. *²²The faithful love of the Lord never ends! His mercies never cease. ²³Great is his faithfulness; his mercies begin afresh each morning. ²⁴I say to myself, "The Lord is my inheritance; therefore, I will hope in him!"²⁵The Lord is good to those who depend on him, to those who search for him. ...⁴⁰Let us test and examine our ways. Let us turn back to the Lord* (Lamentations 3:22-25, 40).

- **Life Purpose App: Expect God to be faithfully loving, merciful, and good to you each day; in return, examine your ways and be faithfully dependent on God.** Many scholars believe that it was Jeremiah who wrote this poem of lamentation, sorrow, and grief as an expression of his sadness over the mounting destruction of the once-powerful kingdom of David and Solomon. He's been called "the weeping prophet" because of his great sorrow over the sins of the people in the darkest times of the Old Testament. In Lamentations 3:48, he writes: *"Tears stream from my eyes because of the destruction of my people!"* This book is a reminder to all people that our faithful God expects repentance and faithfulness. It's also a prayer asking God for restoration.

Take a look at Mother Teresa's quote and ask yourself, "Why is faithfulness to God more important than any future success you dreamed of having?"

I do not pray for success, I ask for faithfulness.

—Mother Teresa, Catholic nun and missionary

MULLING THINGS OVER
(Draw a picture, write a song, journal your thoughts, or tape in a photo or other keepsake related to your life purpose. Or you can do a *brain dump* list of the things causing your mind to wander—as you pray for God to reveal your boldest life purpose.)

EZEKIEL

Ezekiel's Commission: To go to the nation of Israel and tell people what God says.

Background: Ezekiel wrote while he and the other people of Judah were in captivity in Babylon. He warns the people about their rebellion and calls them back to God, and he delivered this message using dramatic, illustrative role-playing scenarios, such as eating a scroll; lying on his left side in a public place with a clay model in front of him; baking his bread over a fire of cow dung; shaving his head and beard, and then burning that hair; and digging through a wall. Ezekiel's message of hope is this: *God will never stop pursuing you!* These two passages focus on God's call of Ezekiel as a messenger and watchman, whose responsibility it was to warn stubborn, hard-hearted, and wicked Israel.

- **Ezekiel's Call and Commission.** *³"Son of man," he [the Spirit] said, "I am **sending** you to the nation of Israel, a rebellious nation that has rebelled against me. They and their ancestors have been rebelling against me to this very day. ⁴They are a stubborn and hard-hearted people. But I am **sending** you to say to them, 'This is what the Sovereign Lord says!' ⁵And whether they listen or refuse to listen—for remember, they are* rebels—*at least they will know they have had a prophet among them"* (Ezekiel 2:3-5, emphases added).

- **A Watchman for Israel.** *[16]After seven days the Lord gave me a message. He said, [17]"Son of man, I have **appointed** you as a watchman for Israel. **Whenever you receive a message from me**, warn people immediately. [18]If I warn the wicked, saying, 'You are under the penalty of death,' but you fail to deliver the warning, they will die in their sins. And I will hold you responsible for their deaths. [19]If you warn them and they refuse to repent and keep on sinning, they will die in their sins. But you will have saved yourself because you obeyed me"* (Ezekiel 3:16-19, emphases added).

Reflection Questions:

1. If, like Ezekiel, you could use a wildly dramatic method to communicate a message of repentance, what might your delivery method look like or sound like? For example, would you sing, dance, mime, juggle, skate, perform, sign, speak, decorate, remodel, sculpt, finger paint, photograph, design, style, or cook?

2. In what way are you, like Ezekiel, commissioned, sent, and appointed as a messenger for God and a watchman (a guard on duty, like in a watchtower) to help warn a certain group of people?

Prayer: God, tell me what delivery method you'd like me to use to communicate my life message. If you feel I need more creativity in my style, just say the word. I want to be the most effective messenger I can be to those I'm called to serve.

MULLING THINGS OVER

(Draw a picture, write a song, journal your thoughts, or tape in a photo or other keepsake related to your life purpose. Or you can do a *brain dump* list of the things causing your mind to wander—as you pray for God to reveal your boldest life purpose.)

DANIEL

Daniel's Purpose in the Face of Persecution: To stand firm in his beliefs and be faithful to God.

Background: Daniel, the most capable and trustworthy administrator of King Darius, was on the fast track to running the entire empire of Babylon. The other staff became jealous and convinced the king to make a law prohibiting prayer to anyone except himself, the king—under penalty of being thrown into a den of lions. After it was reported that Daniel prayed to God, the king couldn't find any loophole in the law to save him from punishment-by-lion. Let this story remind you of how God rescues, saves, and performs miracles for those who are faithful.

- **Daniel in the Lions' Den.** *16So at last the king gave orders for Daniel to be arrested and thrown into the den of lions. The king said to him, "May your God, whom you serve so faithfully, rescue you." 17A stone was brought and placed over the mouth of the den. The king sealed the stone with his own royal seal and the seals of his nobles, so that no one could rescue Daniel. 18Then the king returned to his palace and spent the night fasting. He refused his usual entertainment and couldn't sleep at all that* *night.* ¹⁹*Very early the next morning, the king got up and hurried out to the lions' den.* ²⁰*When he got there, he called out in anguish, "Daniel, servant of the living God! Was your God, whom you serve so faithfully, able to rescue you from the lions?"*

²¹*Daniel answered, "Long live the king!* ²²*My God sent his angel to shut the lions' mouths so that they would not hurt me, for I have been found innocent in his sight. And I have not wronged you, Your Majesty."* ²³*The king was overjoyed and ordered that Daniel be lifted from the den. Not a scratch was found on him, for he had trusted in his God. ...*

²⁵*Then King Darius sent this message to the people of every race and nation and language throughout the world: "Peace and prosperity to you!* ²⁶*I decree that everyone throughout my kingdom should tremble with fear before the God of Daniel. For he is the living God, and he will endure forever. His kingdom will never be destroyed, and his rule will never end.* ²⁷*He rescues and saves his people; he performs miraculous signs and wonders in the heavens and on earth. He has rescued Daniel from the power of the lions"* (Daniel 6:16-23, 25-27).

Reflection Questions:

1. Daniel faced lions instead of bowing to an earthly king who acted like he was a god. What do you think you'd have done in Daniel's situation—and why do you think that?

2. When have you seen God rescue, save, and perform miracles for you or someone else who was faithful? What future miracle would really help you launch as a purpose-filled person?

Prayer: God, I desire to remain faithful to you like Daniel; help me with my unfaithfulness. Help me, too, with my fears and worries, but especially help me overcome my doubt that you'll ever be able to use me for a meaningful and sacred purpose.

DANIEL BONUS ROUND: Check out this story of three men who remained faithful to God by standing firm:

- 3:1-30—**Shadrach, Meshach, and Abednego** (Daniel's three friends) knew they'd be thrown into the fiery furnace if they didn't bow to the ground to worship King Nebuchadnezzar's gold statue. They refused to bow, believing that God would save them from the flames, and that's exactly what happened!

MULLING THINGS OVER
(Draw a picture, write a song, journal your thoughts, or tape in a photo or other keepsake related to your life purpose. Or you can do a *brain dump* list of the things causing your mind to wander—as you pray for God to reveal your boldest life purpose.)

HOSEA

Paths of the Lord. *Let those who are wise understand these things. Let those with discernment listen carefully. The paths of the Lord are true and right, and righteous people live by walking in them. But in those paths sinners stumble and fall (Hosea 14:9).*

- **Life Purpose App: Walk in the paths of the Lord that are true and right.** Being righteous (right-thinking, good, blameless, honorable, honest) means putting one foot in front of the other, day after day, decision after decision, as you walk down the good path that God has laid out for you. What relationships have you invested in with righteous people? Who displays unconditional love when you stumble and fall? Which people can you lean on for wisdom and discernment regarding your life's calling when you grow weary walking down the true and right pathway?

Listen Carefully. Many animals communicate the location of food to other members of their species. For example, the honeybee does a circular or waggle dance to tell other bees the location of a food source, ants leave a scent trail for other ants to follow to the food, and chimps regularly vocalize to communicate the presence of food. Some birds may even screech as they exchange information with other birds about where to find the location of fruit-bearing trees. Similarly, God clearly shares the best faith-walk location with us—calling us to the paths that are true and right. The Bible teaches us how to "listen carefully" to God to find those paths (Hosea 14:9).

MULLING THINGS OVER

(Draw a picture, write a song, journal your thoughts, or tape in a photo or other keepsake related to your life purpose. Or you can do a *brain dump* list of the things causing your mind to wander—as you pray for God to reveal your boldest life purpose.)

JOEL

Salvation. ³¹"The sun will become dark, and the moon will turn blood red before that great and terrible day of the Lord arrives. ³²But everyone who calls on the name of the Lord will be saved,* for some on Mount Zion in Jerusalem will escape, just as the Lord has said. These will be among the survivors whom the Lord has called" (Joel 2:31-32).

*Did you realize that other verses in the Bible refer to this verse?

- **Romans 10:13**—For "Everyone who calls on the name of the Lord will be saved."

- **Acts 2:21**—" 'But everyone who calls on the name of the Lord will be saved.' "

- **Life Purpose App: Call out to God.** The prophet Joel struggled to convince the people of Judah that the plague of locusts that had eaten everything in sight was *nothing* compared to the destruction God would send on their land if they didn't repent. He urged them to choose a life of blessings, of being led by the Holy Spirit, and of miracles, restoration, peace, and prosperity. To Joel, their choice seemed like a no-brainer. What would your daily life be like if you experienced blessings, the power of the Holy Spirit, miracles, restoration, peace, and prosperity? And how would you rank those blessings in priority order for use in the unfolding of your daring and deliberate life mission?

6 Ways to Get Ice Cubes Out of a Tray. (1) Run warm water over the bottom of the tray until you hear the cubes crackle. (2) Place the tray upside down on a cube-catcher and walk away until they have all dropped into the bucket. (3) Pound the trays on the countertop and do whatever it takes to "scare" them out. (4) Ask somebody where to buy recycled rubber trays that have a little stretch to the sides. (5) Hunt for hours online to find and order the trays with the squeeze tabs on the bottom. Frankly, no matter what your strategy, the cubes may or may not come out because ice crumbles. (6) If all else fails, you can save all your extra cash for a bunch of years and get a fancy refrigerator with an ice dispenser.

But there aren't so many options to think about regarding salvation. The Bible tells us that Jesus is the only way. No shortcuts and no tricks to this process. Only Jesus. Have you turned to him for forgiveness?

AMOS

The Lord Speaks. *For the Lord is the one who shaped the mountains, stirs up the winds, and reveals his thoughts to mankind. He turns the light of dawn into darkness and treads on the heights of the earth. The Lord God of Heaven's Armies is his name! (Amos 4:13).*

- **Life Purpose App: If you listen, you can hear God's thoughts.** Don't you wish God would use a modern method of communication, like your cell phone, to speak to you? In the meantime, the old-fashioned method of hearing God's thoughts by just stopping the mind chatter—just being quiet—is still the most effective.

  This idea never ceases to amaze me that God takes the time to communicate with us mere mortals personally. It's truly mind-boggling. Think about what this means in relation to asking God to reveal your most unique life purpose to you! Any thoughts?

A Call to Repentance. *15Hate evil and love what is good; turn your courts into true halls of justice. Perhaps even yet the Lord God of Heaven's Armies will have mercy on the remnant of his people. …23"Away with your noisy hymns of praise! I will not listen to the music of your harps. 24Instead, I want to see a mighty flood of justice, an endless river of righteous living" (Amos 5:15, 23-24).*

- **Life Purpose App: Hate evil and love what is good.** God calls us to righteous living—to hate evil, love what is good, and strive to live a moral, respectable, just, and decent life. Righteousness brings an outpouring (or mighty flood) of justice. Amos, a shepherd and prophet, goes on in Amos 8:4-6 to give a long list of specific examples of *unrighteous* living:

  - Robbing the poor

  - Trampling the needy

  - Wishing for the Sabbath day to be over, so you can sin

  - Cheating the helpless

  - Measuring things dishonestly to cheat the buyer

  - Selling products, like grain, that are purposefully loaded with impurities

  - Enslaving poor people

In what way does a commitment to hate evil and to love what is good help launch you to make your specific, eternal contribution?

Methods of Communication. Mail, e-mail, Facebook®, websites, blogs, voice mail, instant messaging, texting, cell phone, fax, Skype®, videoconferencing, and Flip® videos. What are some of your other favorite methods of catching up with family and friends, or communicating with teachers, coaches, vendors, retail stores, e-commerce companies, health care providers, airlines, hotels, restaurants, utility companies, and computer trouble-shooters halfway around the world?

MULLING THINGS OVER

(Draw a picture, write a song, journal your thoughts, or tape in a photo or other keepsake related to your life purpose. Or you can do a *brain dump* list of the things causing your mind to wander—as you pray for God to reveal your boldest life purpose.)

OBADIAH

Pride Is Punished. *3 "You have been deceived by your own pride because you live in a rock fortress and make your home high in the mountains. 'Who can ever reach us way up here?' you ask boastfully. 4But even if you soar as high as eagles and build your nest among the stars, I will bring you crashing down,"* says the Lord (Obadiah 1:3-4).

- **Life Purpose App: Don't be deceived by pride; don't boast.** When the people of Judah were torn from their homeland and taken into Babylonian captivity, the Edomites swarmed in and looted what was left behind. In warning the godless nation Edom that it would be punished for its pride, God gave this harsh reprimand: *"You should not have gloated when they exiled your relatives to distant lands. You should not have rejoiced when the people of Judah suffered such misfortune. You should not have spoken arrogantly in that terrible time of trouble"* (Obadiah 1:12). How could they kick the people of Judah when they were down? How could they harm those who were already suffering calamity? How do pride, arrogance, and gloating get a foothold in someone's life? And how much damage do you think pride, gloating, arrogance, and its sister sin of mistreating others could do to your future mission that's intended for such incredible good?

MULLING THINGS OVER

(Draw a picture, write a song, journal your thoughts, or tape in a photo or other keepsake related to your life purpose. Or you can do a *brain dump* list of the things causing your mind to wander—as you pray for God to reveal your boldest life purpose.)

The only conquests which are permanent, and leave no regrets, are our conquests over ourselves.

—Napoleon Bonaparte, French emperor

JONAH

Jonah's Mission: To go to the great city of Nineveh and announce God's judgment against it.

Background: Jonah had a direct calling from God that he didn't want to answer. So, he fled on a ship bound for Tarshish, instead of heading to Nineveh where he was supposed to go warn more than 120,000 people living in spiritual darkness about their need to repent. After a big fish swallowed him and then spit him out, Jonah finally went on his assigned mission, and the Ninevites repented! Yet Jonah then selfishly got angry at the Lord's mercy on the people and complained and pouted in Jonah 4:3: *"Just kill me now, Lord."*

- **Jonah Runs From the Lord.** *¹The Lord gave this message to Jonah son of Amittai: ²"Get up and go to the great city of Nineveh. Announce my judgment against it because I have seen how wicked its people are." ³But Jonah got up and went in the opposite direction to get away from the Lord. He went down to the port of Joppa, where he found a ship leaving for Tarshish. He bought a ticket and went on board, hoping to escape from the Lord by sailing to Tarshish (Jonah 1:1-3).*

Reflection Questions:

1. Would you have wanted to be Jonah and hear directly and unrelentingly from God? In what way have you (or a friend or family member) heard God speak clearly? Was there obedience involved, or do you recall someone fleeing the scene?

2. What big life assignment from God would you run toward? flee from? Why?

Prayer: God, I struggle with being stubborn and selfish like Jonah. Help me obey without you needing to take drastic measures to convince me that you know best. In other words, help me not to "pull a Jonah." I'd sure like to avoid a "big fish scene" and the poor reputation that goes along with it!

MICAH

What is Good? *No, O people, the Lord has told you what is good, and this is what he requires of you: to do what is right, to love mercy, and to walk humbly with your God (Micah 6:8).*

- **Life Purpose App: Do what's right, love mercy, and walk humbly with God.** God's requirements of doing right and being good are easier said than done. What step can you take now toward making this Micah 6:8 mindset a basic premise—a vital component—of your life's work? Or do you feel that it sets way too high a standard for your already challenging assignment?

Tough Assignments. Which is harder: learning to snowboard or ski? doing a front handspring or back handspring? taking an ACT or SAT exam? studying physics or chemistry? applying Micah 6:8 to your daily life or fulfilling your unique life purpose without God's help?

MULLING THINGS OVER

(Draw a picture, write a song, journal your thoughts, or tape in a photo or other keepsake related to your life purpose. Or you can do a *brain dump* list of the things causing your mind to wander—as you pray for God to reveal your boldest life purpose.)

NAHUM

Strong Refuge. *The Lord is good, a strong refuge when trouble comes. He is close to those who trust in him (Nahum 1:7).*

- **Life Purpose App: Trust God at all times, including when trouble comes.** When you trust people completely, you trust them to *be who they say they are* and *do what they say they'll do.* You also trust them to love you unconditionally and have your best interest at heart at all times. Do you trust God to be good to you and to be a strong refuge when trouble comes? Do you really believe that God loves you unconditionally and has your best interest at heart at all times? In what way have you felt God's goodness (such as through God's protection, provision, power, faithfulness, compassion, guidance, gentleness, grace), especially in relation to your complex, long-term mission?

God's Handiwork. Few architectural works of art compare to the Eiffel Tower in Paris. It was built in 1889, and today it's the world's most visited monument with an entrance free. Three-hundred workers joined together 18,038 pieces of puddled iron, using 2.5 million rivets[5] to build the tower that stands as tall as an 81-story building. The risk of accident during construction was great because of the open frame, but only one worker died.[6] But France's global icon pales in comparison to who you are: God's far more valuable and magnificent creation, a precious work of art obviously worth dying for. Your only real purpose has been riveted into your soul: to stand tall in your God-designed temple, trusting your Maker, your Savior with your life.

MULLING THINGS OVER

(Draw a picture, write a song, journal your thoughts, or tape in a photo or other keepsake related to your life purpose. Or you can do a *brain dump* list of the things causing your mind to wander—as you pray for God to reveal your boldest life purpose.)

HABAKKUK

The Lord's Reply to Habakkuk: *The Lord replied, "Look around at the nations; look and be amazed! For I am doing something in your own day, something you wouldn't believe even if someone told you about it"* (Habakkuk 1:5).

- **Life Purpose App: Be amazed at the miracles God has planned for you.**

The Lord's Second Reply. *²Then the Lord said to me, "Write my answer plainly on tablets, so that a runner can carry the correct message to others. ³This vision is for a future time. It describes the end, and it will be fulfilled. If it seems slow in coming, wait patiently, for it will surely take place. It will not be delayed"* (Habakkuk 2:2-3).

- **Life Purpose App: Share the vision God gives you with others, even if it seems slow in unfolding.**

Habakkuk's Prayer. *¹⁶I will wait quietly for the coming day when disaster will strike the people who invade us. ¹⁷Even though the fig trees have no blossoms, and there are no grapes on the vines; even though the olive crop fails, and the fields lie empty and barren; even though the flocks die in the fields, and the cattle barns are empty, ¹⁸yet I will rejoice in the Lord! I will be joyful in the God of my salvation! (Habakkuk 3:16-18).*

- **Life Purpose App: Rejoice in the Lord, even when it's hard to wait for the triumphal end of the story.**

SUMMARY QUESTIONS FOR HABAKKUK: As the Judeans were falling into the hands of the invading Babylonian army and being exiled, they frantically asked, "Where's God?" The prophet Habakkuk told them that God had assured him that this terrifying time wasn't the end of their story—that the bigger picture was one of hope. What do these three practical applications suggest as your next step toward being and doing all God intended? Will you take that next step?

- Be amazed at the miracles God has planned for you.

- Share the vision God gives you with others, even if it seems slow in unfolding. [**Word of caution here:** In the early development of your vision, share only with people you trust.]

- Rejoice in the Lord, even though it's hard to wait for the triumphal end of the story.

ZEPHANIAH

A Call to Repentance. *Seek the Lord, all who are humble, and follow his commands. Seek to do what is right and to live humbly. Perhaps even yet the Lord will protect you—protect you from his anger on that day of destruction (Zephaniah 2:3).*

- **Life Purpose App: Follow God's commands, do what's right, and live humbly.** Zephaniah had to warn God's people about the coming judgment for their sin, but he also got to prophesy about the coming of the Messiah, who'd live among them. This verse serves as a reminder of what curbs God's anger.

With that specific path of repentance spelled out, the prophet continues in Zephaniah 3:14-20 to deliver a message of hope by listing all that God planned to do for the repentant remnant of Israel. He told them to expect that their enemies would be dispersed; their troubles would be over; the Lord himself—the King of Israel—would live among them; they'd never again fear disaster; a mighty Savior would take delight in them and calm their fears; their oppressors would be dealt with severely; the weak and helpless ones would be rescued; the former exiles would be brought back home with glory and fame; they'd receive a good name of distinction; and their fortunes would be restored. Wow! That's quite a list.

Do you realize, though, that even if God never promised to do any of those good things to protect you or your life purpose from destruction, your general purpose in life would still require you to follow God's commands, do what's right, and live humbly? But how wonderful to know that our loving God does want to reward you with a long list of blessings. How would any three of those particular promises of God make it easier for you to fulfill your difficult and targeted purpose in life?

Success is simple. Do what's right, the right way, at the right time.

~ Arnold H. Glasgow, American humorist, 1905-1998

HAGGAI

Success. The Lord *sent this second message to Haggai: "But when this happens, says the Lord of Heaven's Armies, I will honor you, Zerubbabel son of Shealtiel, my servant. I will make you like a signet ring on my finger, says the Lord, for I have chosen you. I, the Lord of Heaven's Armies, have spoken!" (Haggai 2:23).*

- **Life Purpose App: True success is being God's servant.** Zerubbabel, governor of Judah, defined success as *being God's servant.* Overseer of the temple rebuilding project, he was compared to the Lord's signet ring, which was a symbol of honor, authority, and power. How have you defined success in the past? How do you feel about the governor's definition of success?

The Lord's Signet Ring. The world's heaviest gold ring is the Star of Taiba. Mounted with precious stones that are set on a 21-carat gold ring that weights more than a hundred pounds, it's too large to be worn and must sit in a display case to be admired. It is a symbol of extreme wealth and worldly success.[7] On the other hand, the Lord's signet ring (signet from Latin "signum," meaning sign) symbolizes that God's honor, authority, and power rest fully with the person wearing it. It indicates that they have the Lord's distinctive personal signature or seal of approval on their life. Honestly, which ring would you rather have: the Star of Taiba or the Lord's signet ring? Why?

ANOTHER GREAT PURPOSE PASSAGE IN HAGGAI:

- **2:4-5**—[4]" *'But now the Lord says: Be strong, all you people still left in the land. And now get to work, for I am with you, says the Lord of Heaven's Armies. [5]My Spirit remains among you, just as I promised when you came out of Egypt. So do not be afraid.' "*

ZECHARIAH

Zechariah's Mission: To tell the Israelites to get themselves ready and get back to work on the Temple before the Messiah returns.

Background: God gave Zechariah eight visions to deliver to the people of Israel. Among those prophecies, Zechariah shared that the Messiah would be coming soon—humbly riding on a donkey's colt into Jerusalem. He even predicted that the Messiah would come a second time—as a King who'd rule forever. He also warned the Israelites that they needed to work hard to rebuild the Temple and get themselves ready by being humble, fair, merciful, kind, and generous.

- **Get Back to Work.** *⁹"This is what the Lord of Heaven's Armies says: Be strong and finish the task! …¹²For I am planting seeds of peace and prosperity among you. The grapevines will be heavy with fruit. The earth will produce its crops, and the heavens will release the dew. Once more I will cause the remnant in Judah and Israel to inherit these blessings. ¹³Among the other nations, Judah and Israel became symbols of a cursed nation. But no longer! Now I will rescue you and make you both a symbol and a source of blessing. So don't be afraid. Be strong, and get on with rebuilding the Temple!" (Zechariah 8:9, 12-13).*

Reflection Questions:

1. Would it be good or bad news for you if Jesus came back right now?
    In what way would you still like to get your character ready for Jesus'
    return?

2. Like the Israelites who were instructed to *get on with rebuilding the
    Temple*, what one step can you take now toward your most intentional
    life assignment?

Prayer: God, thank you for the advance warning that I need to get myself ready
for your return and complete the "One Big Thing" for which you've wired me. I
pray that my time of preparation for your return will glorify you.

*I count him braver who overcomes his desires than him who conquers his
enemies; for the hardest victory is over self.*

—Aristotle, Greek philosopher

MALACHI

Pour Out a Blessing. *"Bring all the tithes into the storehouse so there will be enough food in my Temple. If you do," says the Lord of Heaven's Armies, "I will open the windows of heaven for you. I will pour out a blessing so great you won't have enough room to take it in! Try it! Put me to the test! ¹¹Your crops will be abundant, for I will guard them from insects and disease. Your grapes will not fall from the vine before they are ripe," says the Lord of Heaven's Armies. ¹²"Then all nations will call you blessed, for your land will be such a delight," says the Lord of Heaven's Armies (Malachi 3:10-12).*

- **Life Purpose App: Bring your tithes to God for the kingdom work that needs to be done.** How do you feel about God's tithing challenge in verse 10: *"Try it! Put me to the test!"*? Have you ever tried to "out-give" God by giving more than the required 10 percent tithe? How would you like to be in the position to do "reverse tithing," which means giving back 90 percent of your income? It sounds wild, but some people actually do that! Or how would you feel about tithing 10 percent and then reserving an additional sum each week to help fund your urgent life's work?

The Coming Day of Judgment. *²"But for you who fear my name, the Sun of Righteousness will rise with healing in his wings. And you will go free, leaping with joy like calves let out to pasture. ³On the day when I act, you will tread upon the wicked as if they were dust under your feet," says the Lord of Heaven's Armies. ⁴"Remember to obey the Law of Moses, my servant—all the decrees and regulations that I gave him on Mount Sinai for all Israel"* (Malachi 4:2-4).

- **Life Purpose App: Obey all of God's commandments.** Have you reviewed and reflected on the Ten Commandments lately? (See list below.) Which commandment causes you the most headache and heartache—the one that could most easily get in the way of you honoring God's intentional design for your life?

> **No Easy Commandments Among the Big Ten!** Here's a quick glance at the list, if you'd like to refresh your memory: I am the Lord your God. You shall have no other gods before me. You shall not make for yourself an idol. You shall not make wrongful use of the name of your God. Remember the Sabbath and keep it holy. Honor your father and mother. You shall not murder. You shall not commit adultery. You shall not steal. You shall not bear false witness against your neighbor. You shall not covet your neighbor's wife. You shall not covet anything that belongs to your neighbor.

PART 2

NEW
TESTAMENT

MATTHEW

Joseph's Purposeful Journey: To protect Jesus from Herod by taking his family out of Bethlehem to Egypt.

Background: Egypt had been a harsh home previously for the Israelites when they lived there as slaves back in the Old Testament, yet in this New Testament moment, it would be a place of refuge for Jesus, Mary, and Joseph, who needed to escape King Herod's slaughter of male infants in Bethlehem. Egypt was approximately 60 miles away from the danger, and it was the closest Roman province that was independent of the king.

- **The Escape to Egypt.** *13After the wise men were gone, an angel of the Lord appeared to Joseph in a dream. "Get up! Flee to Egypt with the child and his mother," the angel said. "Stay there until I tell you to return, because Herod is going to search for the child to kill him." 14That night Joseph left for Egypt with the child and Mary, his mother, 15and they stayed there until Herod's death. This fulfilled what the Lord had spoken through the prophet: "I called my Son out of Egypt" (Matthew 2:13-15).*

Reflection Questions:

1. What person, place, or thing do you need to flee from or run toward to protect Jesus in your heart and protect the passionate ache God has put in your heart?

2. Verse 14 says that Joseph headed to Egypt with his family that night, even though he'd been fast asleep before he got the instructions. What's the longest or shortest amount of time it's taken you to obey God in a situation? How will a shorter **Hear + Obey** lag time help you accomplish your God-orchestrated dream more efficiently and effectively?

Prayer: God, it took great faith and courage for Joseph and Mary to flee in the middle of the night with Jesus. Please grant me a generous portion of courage and faith that I'll need to flee from danger and run toward a life of significance.

MATTHEW BONUS ROUND: Check out these examples of what's required of people called to do God's will on earth:

- 2:1-12—**The three kings** were wealthy magi who brought gifts to Jesus and were given the gift, in return, of recognizing and worshipping Christ the King. They obeyed God, who warned them in a dream not to return to Herod.

- 14:28-33—**Peter** obeyed Jesus by getting out of the boat and walking on water, even though his fear caught up with him.

- 16:18—**Peter** (also known as Simon Peter) was told by Jesus: *"Now I say to you that you are Peter (which means 'rock'), and upon this rock I will build my church, and all the powers of hell will not conquer it."*

- 26:6-13—**Mary of Bethany** anointed Jesus with oil—an act of worship that Jesus said would be discussed worldwide; she isn't named here, but John 12:1-8 identifies Mary of Bethany as the woman who performed this act of worship.

- 26:39—**Jesus** surrendered to God, when crying out in the Garden of Gethsemane, *"I want your will to be done, not mine."*

MULLING THINGS OVER
(Draw a picture, write a song, journal your thoughts, or tape in a photo or other keepsake related to your life purpose. Or you can do a *brain dump* list of the things causing your mind to wander—as you pray for God to reveal your boldest life purpose.)

MARK

The Optimal Timing for Answering the Call: To respond immediately when Jesus commands, "Come follow me."

Background: Jesus called Simon, Andrew, James, and John, who were rough, unschooled, Galilean fishermen, to an all-new life of evangelism training, influence, and discipling. Take their stories as an encouragement that when Jesus calls you to a specific position or role in life, you only need to be willing to yield to and learn from the Master to be successful. You aren't responsible for dreaming up the vision and knowing beforehand how to do each task.

- **The First Disciples.** *[16]One day as Jesus was walking along the shore of the Sea of Galilee, he saw Simon and his brother Andrew throwing a net into the water, for they fished for a living. [17]Jesus called out to them, "Come, follow me, and I will show you how to fish for people!" [18]And they left their nets at once and followed him. [19]A little farther up the shore Jesus saw Zebedee's sons, James and John, in a boat repairing their nets. [20]He called them at once, and they also followed him, leaving their father, Zebedee, in the boat with the hired men (Mark 1:16-20).*

Reflection Questions:

1. If tomorrow you were out fishing, wading in the water, repairing a boat, or walking along your favorite shoreline, and you heard Jesus call out to you—*"Come, follow me, and I will show you how to fish for people!"*—what would your response be, and why?

2. Do you think God wants to send people, like the four fishermen, to help you with the biggest assignment of your life? Imagine yourself saying something like this to those people God may be calling to help you: *God has entrusted me with a ministry to_____. Will you help me? We'll need to rely heavily on the power of God to work through us.* If not these words, what words might you use to enlist a group of people who can support you?

Prayer: God, for all the times I've ignored your personal and urgent call on my life, forgive me. Thank you for reminding me of the immediate response of the first disciples. I, too, want to follow you wherever you lead.

MARK BONUS ROUND: Check out these stories about being sent, chosen, and called:

- 6:7-13—**The Twelve Disciples** were sent out by Jesus in pairs, with authority to cast out evil spirits. They told everyone to repent and turn to God.

- 10:46-52—**Bartimaeus**, a blind man, begged Jesus for mercy and a miracle. Jesus told the crowd, *"Tell him to come here,"* so the people relayed the message to the blind man, *"Come on, he's calling you!"* (v. 49). That day, Bartimaeus received the gifts of sight and salvation by responding to Jesus' call.

- 15:21—**Simon of Cyrene**, a man from North Africa, was conscripted, drafted, called up, "chosen at random" by Roman guards to help Jesus carry the cross to Golgotha. (Does God *do random*? No!)

Great Dane, the Gentle Giant. Scooby-Doo and Marmaduke romp around as two fictional Great Danes the world loves to read about and watch. But Giant George, a real-life, blue Great Dane, measures 43 inches high at the shoulders and weighs in at 245 pounds. This gentle giant bounded into this world in November 2005 and resides now in Tucson, Arizona. Currently, he ranks as the world's tallest-ever dog, according to Guinness World Records and *The Oprah Winfrey Show*, where he was a guest in February 2010. What a crazy, fun day that must have been in the studio! Giant George apparently sleeps in a queen-sized bed and enjoys his hobby of being driven around his neighborhood in a golf cart. What about you? Regardless of your height and weight, your hobbies, or your favorite method of transportation, are you a gentle giant who's setting the bar high with your love for God?

MULLING THINGS OVER

(Draw a picture, write a song, journal your thoughts, or tape in a photo or other keepsake related to your life purpose. Or you can do a *brain dump* list of the things causing your mind to wander—as you pray for God to reveal your boldest life purpose.)

LUKE

The Lord's Plan For Mary: To conceive, as a virgin, through the power of the Most High, and to give birth to a son who'd be named Jesus.

Background: Mary's life changed forever the day the angel Gabriel appeared to her with the news that she'd conceive and give birth to a son who would be the promised Savior. When Mary surrendered her life plans that day, knowing that she could be stoned to death for being pregnant out of wedlock, she was agreeing to be used for God's glory.

- **Mary Responds to God's Call.** *²⁶In the sixth month of Elizabeth's pregnancy, God sent the angel Gabriel to Nazareth, a village in Galilee, ²⁷to a virgin named Mary. She was engaged to be married to a man named Joseph, a descendant of King David. ²⁸Gabriel appeared to her and said, "Greetings, favored woman! The Lord is with you!" ²⁹Confused and disturbed, Mary tried to think what the angel could mean. ³⁰"Don't be afraid, Mary," the angel told her, "for you have found favor with ___ ___ will conceive and give birth to a son, and you will name ___ ___ ll be very great and will be called the Son of the Most ___ ll give him the throne of his ancestor David. ___ forever; his Kingdom will never end!"*

³⁴Mary asked the angel, "But how can this happen? I am a virgin."
³⁵The angel replied, "The Holy Spirit will come upon you, and the power of the Most High will overshadow you. So the baby to be born will be holy, and he will be called the Son of God. ³⁶What's more, your relative Elizabeth has become pregnant in her old age! People used to say she was barren, but she's now in her sixth month. ³⁷For nothing is impossible with God." ³⁸Mary responded, "I am the Lord's servant. May everything you have said about me come true." And then the angel left her (Luke 1:26-38).

Reflection Questions:

1. How difficult do you think it was for Mary to fulfill her God-created role? What character trait do you think she needed most for her job, and why?

2. What huge life assignment do you fear most for yourself, and why? Do you believe God will insist on giving you that particular mega-task?

Prayer: God, you only assign impossible tasks so that your glory may be evident to all who witness the miracles you orchestrate. Cure me of my fear of the impossible.

LUKE BONUS ROUND: Check out these stories of willing people who were chosen for work that brought glory to God:

- 1:1-17, 67-79—**Zechariah**, a man who was righteous (good) in God's eyes, was chosen by God to be the father of John the Baptist. When his son was 8 days old, Zechariah prophesized through the power of the Holy Spirit that John would prepare the way for the Lord.

- 1:6-7, 57—**Elizabeth**, the wife of Zechariah who also was righteous in God's eyes, had been unable to conceive a child. God chose her in her old age to be the mother of John the Baptist.

- 1:13-17—**John the Baptist**, who was *filled with the Holy Spirit, even before his birth* (v. 15), was chosen by God to prepare people for the coming of the Lord.

- 2:25-35—**Simeon**, a devout man led by the Holy Spirit, had been eagerly waiting for the Messiah to rescue Israel. He felt led to go to the Temple the day Jesus was presented to the Lord by Mary and Joseph— and God chose Simeon to deliver a great prophecy about the Child.

- 2:36-38—**Anna**, a prophetess and widow, lived in the Temple day and night, worshipping God with fasting and prayer. She came along just as Simeon was talking with Mary and Joseph, and God chose her to tell others about the child who'd one day rescue Jerusalem.

- 19:1-10—**Zacchaeus**, a short, rich man and the chief tax collector of the Jericho region, was singled out from a crowd by Jesus and was chosen to host a meal in his home. Zacchaeus believed in Jesus that day and repented of his sins.

- 23:39-43—**One of the criminals on a cross**, who reprimanded his fellow criminal for not fearing God, was chosen to be a powerful witness to the world that day and for all generations to come. He spoke the truth that was revealed to him about Christ, and his faith was rewarded with the privilege of a personal invitation to live with Jesus in paradise that very day.

JOHN

Jesus' Purpose for Peter: To shepherd the church's flock.

Background: When Peter confessed that Jesus was the Son of the living God, he was given a colossal responsibility: to take care of the new church's flock. Wouldn't you know it, though, he still denied Christ three times before Jesus' crucifixion. Later, Jesus graciously gave Peter three opportunities to profess his love again—and the disciple accepted the opportunity for the do-over. This time, as soon as Peter heard what struggles he'd face in his future for the glory of God, he tried to get the inside scoop to compare his assignment with what God had planned for the disciple John's future. Jesus' reply was classic: *"What is that to you? As for you, follow me" (John 21:22).*

- **Feed my lambs.** *15After breakfast Jesus asked Simon Peter, "Simon son of John, do you love me more than these?" "Yes, Lord," Peter replied, "you know I love you." "Then feed my lambs," Jesus told him. 16Jesus repeated the question: "Simon son of John, do you love me?" "Yes, Lord," Peter said, "you know I love you." "Then take care of my sheep," Jesus said. 17A third time he asked him, "Simon son of John, do you love me?" Peter was hurt that Jesus asked the question a third time. He said, "Lord, you know everything. You know that I love you." Jesus said, "Then feed my sheep."*

101

18 "I tell you the truth, when you were young, you were able to do as you liked; you dressed yourself and went wherever you wanted to go. But when you are old, you will stretch out your hands, and others will dress you and take you where you don't want to go." 19 Jesus said this to let him know by what kind of death he would glorify God. Then Jesus told him, "Follow me."

20 Peter turned around and saw behind them the disciple Jesus loved— the one who had leaned over to Jesus during supper and asked, "Lord, who will betray you?" 21 Peter asked Jesus, "What about him, Lord?" 22 Jesus replied, "If I want him to remain alive until I return, what is that to you? As for you, follow me" (John 21:15-22).

Reflection Questions:

1. If Jesus asked you, *"(insert your first name)* _____, do you love me more than these?"*—how would you respond and why?

2. In what way could jealousy of another person's life or grand purpose prevent you from obeying God's plan for you—or cause you to do so with a reluctant or bitter heart?

Prayer: God, I love you more every day for who you are. Thank you for the joy I have in you, in my relationships, and in my custom-fitted mission. Forgive me for all the times I've denied you or been jealous of the life you've designed for others.

JOHN BONUS ROUND: Check out these stories of Jesus calling people to a new life and a new reality:

- 1:43—**Philip**, whom Jesus found in Galilee, was told, *"Come, follow me."*

- 1:45-51—**Nathanael** was called *"a man of complete integrity"* (v. 47) and became a disciple when he declared Jesus to be *"the Son of God— the King of Israel"* (v. 49).

- 4:1-42—**The Samaritan Woman**, a nameless divorcee who'd had five husbands and was living with a man at the time, heard Jesus say, *"I Am the Messiah!"* (v. 26). She immediately began to share the news with her entire town.

- 20:11-18—**Mary Magdalene** obeyed Jesus when instructed to deliver a post-Resurrection message to the disciples. She began with, *"I have seen the Lord!"* (v. 18).

JOHN

My Father's Will. *Jesus replied, "For I [Jesus] have come down from heaven to do the will of God who sent me, not to do my own will" (John 6:38).*

- **Life Purpose App: Follow Jesus' example and do the will of God.**

Act With Urgency. Jesus answered, *"We must quickly carry out the tasks assigned us by the one who sent us. The night is coming, and then no one can work" (John 9:4).*

- **Life Purpose App: Quickly carry out the tasks God assigns you.**

The Good Shepherd. Jesus explained, *"The thief's purpose is to steal and kill and destroy. My purpose is to give them [my sheep] a rich and satisfying life" (John 10:10).*

- **Life Purpose App: Enjoy and express gratitude for the truth that Jesus' purpose is to give you a rich and satisfying life!**

Produce Lasting Fruit. Jesus replied, *"You didn't choose me. I chose you. I appointed you to go and produce lasting fruit, so that the Father will give you whatever you ask for, using my name" (John 15:16).*

- **Life Purpose App: Go and produce the lasting fruit that Jesus appointed you to produce.**

Give All Glory to God. Jesus looked up to heaven and said, *"I brought glory to you here on earth by completing the work you gave me to do"* (John 17:4).

- **Life Purpose App: Bring glory to God by completing your work here on earth.**

Go Into the World. Jesus prayed, *"In the same way that you gave me a mission in the world, I give them a mission in the world"* (John 17:18 The Message).

- **Life Purpose App: Accept your mission in the world.**

SUMMARY QUESTIONS FOR JOHN: What do these six practical applications suggest as a next step for you toward your most invigorating, exhausting, and dramatic life purpose? Will you take that step?

- Follow Jesus' example and do the will of God.

- Quickly carry out the tasks God assigns you.

- Enjoy and express gratitude for the truth that Jesus' purpose is to give you a rich and satisfying life!

- Go and produce the lasting fruit that Jesus appointed you to produce.

- Bring glory to God by completing your work here on earth.

- Accept your mission in the world.

Good works do not make a good man, but a good man does good works.

—Martin Luther, German theologian who initiated the Protestant Reformation

MULLING THINGS OVER

(Draw a picture, write a song, journal your thoughts, or tape in a photo or other keepsake related to your life purpose. Or you can do a *brain dump* list of the things causing your mind to wander—as you pray for God to reveal your boldest life purpose.)

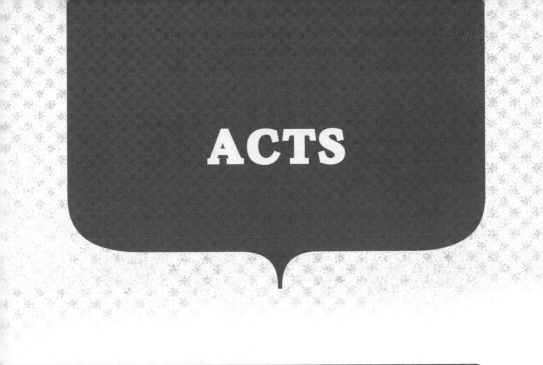

ACTS

Digging deeper into... Acts 8:26-31, 35-39

Philip's Mission: To share the good news of the gospel with the treasurer of Ethiopia.

Background: Philip, an evangelist, was one of the seven men chosen by the apostles to serve the early church by ministering to the Greek-speaking widows and the poor. In this particular passage, God gave him a new short-term, targeted assignment, which was to *go south down the desert road* and *walk along beside the carriage*. When Philip went and asked the stranger in the carriage if he understood what he was reading in Isaiah, the man said no. So Philip rode along explaining the Scripture, and he agreed to baptize the man. Afterward, Philip disappeared into thin air. Now *that's* a mission with flair!

- **Philip is Called to the Ethiopian.** *²⁶As for Philip, an angel of the Lord said to him, "Go south down the desert road that runs from Jerusalem to Gaza." ²⁷So he started out, and he met the treasurer of Ethiopia, a eunuch of great authority under the Kandake, the queen of Ethiopia. The eunuch had gone to Jerusalem to worship, ²⁸and he was now returning. Seated in his carriage, he was reading aloud from the book of the prophet Isaiah. ²⁹The Holy Spirit said to Philip, "Go over and walk along beside the carriage." ³⁰Philip ran over and heard the man reading* *from the prophet Isaiah. Philip asked, "Do you understand what you are reading?"* [31] *The man replied, "How can I, unless someone instructs me?"* ...

[35] *So beginning with this same Scripture, Philip told him the Good News about Jesus.* [36] *As they rode along, they came to some water, and the eunuch said, "Look! There's some water! Why can't I be baptized?"* [37] *He ordered the carriage to stop, and they went down into the water, and Philip baptized him.* [38] *When they came up out of the water, the Spirit of the Lord snatched Philip away. The eunuch never saw him again but went on his way rejoicing (Acts 8:26-31, 35-38).*

Reflection Questions:

1. If, unlike Philip, you actually got to choose your ministry audience, whom might you choose? For example, would you like to minister to actors, atheists, athletes, cancer patients, children, high school students, disabled veterans, drug addicts, educators, engaged couples, immigrants, law enforcement officers, military families, pastors, politicians, prisoners, the elderly, widows, youth leaders, or an international people-group?

    How do you feel about sharing the good news at home or abroad— or inviting someone to discuss a particular step, like repentance or surrender? In what way is any or all of that part of your calling?

Prayer: God, I'm torn between wanting to hear you say "Go" to a specific place to serve, versus wanting to do my own thing in my own hometown. Tell me specifically whom you'd like me to serve. Help me realize that my true joy and peace will come from gladly going wherever you send me.

ACTS BONUS ROUND: Check out these stories of people who lived purposeful lives:

- 7:54-60—**Stephen** was given the rare and beautiful, spiritual gift of martyrdom. He spoke boldly and was willing to die for Jesus. His accusers killed him with stones.

- 9:1-22—**Saul**, a notorious persecutor of Christians, became a brand-new man when Jesus called him on the road to Damascus. Saul's preaching in the name of Christ became a powerful influence from that time forward.

- 11:24-26—**Barnabas**, a good man of strong faith who was guided by the Holy Spirit, felt called to mentor and encourage Saul (soon to be known as Paul) for a full year in Antioch. Saul needed the Antioch church, at that time, as a place to help him develop trusted relationships and a respected teaching ministry.

- 16:13-15—**Lydia**, a successful businesswoman who sold expensive purple cloth, listened to Paul's words one day on a riverbank. God opened her heart, and she became the first recorded convert to Christ in Europe. She valued her faith so much that she hosted the new church that was formed in the city of Philippi.

Why Was Saul's Name Changed to Paul?

Yes, it's true that God did change the disciple Simon's name to the Greek name, Petros (Peter); however, God didn't change Saul's name to Paul. Here's the scoop on Saul-Paul!

Fact: Saul of Tarsus was an Israelite/Hebrew/Jew born probably two years after Jesus. His parents gave him the Hebrew name Saul and sent him as a young teenager to attend a Pharisaic Rabbinical school that demanded the strictest obedience to Jewish law.

Fact: Because his father was a Roman citizen, Saul inherited Roman citizenship at birth, and he was also given the Latin name Paul at that time.

Fact: After his conversion, Saul was called by God to bring the gospel to the Gentiles, so shortly thereafter (in Acts 13:9), Saul began to use his Roman name Paul, a name familiar to Gentiles that would help put them at ease with his message and jaw-dropping faith story.

ACTS

Listening to the Holy Spirit. *²²"And now I [Paul] am bound by the Spirit to go to Jerusalem. I don't know what awaits me, ²³except that the Holy Spirit tells me in city after city that jail and suffering lie ahead. ²⁴But my life is worth nothing to me unless I use it for finishing the work assigned me by the Lord Jesus—the work of telling others the Good News about the wonderful grace of God" (Acts 20:22-24).*

- **Life Purpose App: Finish the work assigned you. One of the basic, universal purposes in life for all Christians is to tell others** *"the Good News about the wonderful grace of God" (Acts 20:24).* To do this in your own unique way as planned by God, what help do you need? Answer that question as if it's Jesus asking you and wanting to launch you: "My dear one, what do you need?"

Doing God's Will. *"After David had done the will of God in his own generation, he died and was buried with his ancestors, and his body decayed"* (Acts 13:36).

Life Purpose App: Do the will of God. What's more important in life than doing the will of God before you die? Why do you think that?

OTHER GREAT PURPOSE PASSAGES IN ACTS:

- 2:23—*"But God knew what would happen, and his prearranged plan was carried out when Jesus was betrayed."*

- 4:27-28—[27]*"In fact, this has happened here in this very city! For Herod Antipas, Pontius Pilate the governor, the Gentiles, and the people of Israel were all united against Jesus, your holy servant, whom you anointed. [28]But everything they did was determined beforehand according to your will."*

- 17:26-28—[26]*"From one man he created all the nations throughout the whole earth. He decided beforehand when they should rise and fall, and he determined their boundaries. [27]His purpose was for the nations to seek after God and perhaps feel their way toward him and find him— though he is not far from any one of us. [28]For in him we live and move and exist."*

Answering the Call. In 1935, Mr. Willy Müller invented the first automatic answering machine for telephone messages. The device was 3 feet tall and was popular with Orthodox Jews who were forbidden to answer the phone on the Sabbath.[8] What can you do now to ensure you'll hear God's call on your life—and answer it? Or would you rather the message go to your voice mail, so you can delete it and ignore it if you don't like the assignment?

ROMANS

Good Trumps Evil. *And we know that God causes everything to work together for the good of those who love God and are called according to his purpose for them (Romans 8:28).*

- **Life Purpose App: God causes all things in a Christian's life to work together for good.** God is a master at taking evil (that was caused by our fallen world or intended by the devil) and miraculously resurrecting some measure of hope out of it. In what circumstance has God shown up to create something good out of evil for you or for a loved one? How could that experience begin to enrich your most dramatic life purpose?

Spiritual Gifts. *In his grace, God has given us different gifts for doing certain things well (Romans 12:6).*

- **Life Purpose App: God promises to equip you with particular spiritual gifts to help you complete your life mission.** God gives Christians a variety of spiritual gifts to use in their daily tasks to bless the body of Christ and also to use with their most distinct life mission.

Identify one or two of these gifts you think you might have that other mature Christians would affirm in you: leadership, encouragement, intercessory prayer, faith, mercy, service/helps, pastor/shepherd, speaking/preaching, writing, giving financially, evangelism, discipleship, healing, hospitality, discernment, administration/organization, prophecy (blessed sayings), modern missionary/apostle, wisdom, knowledge, martyrdom. If you haven't talked with anyone yet about your giftedness, it's a great conversation to have!

OTHER GREAT PURPOSE PASSAGES IN ROMANS:

- **9:11-12**—*[11]But before they [Esau and Jacob] were born, before they had done anything good or bad, she [Rebekah] received a message from God. (This message shows that God chooses people according to his own purposes; [12]he calls people, but not according to their good or bad works.) She was told, "Your older son will serve your younger son."*

- **13:4**—*The authorities are God's servants, sent for your good. But if you are doing wrong, of course you should be afraid, for they have the power to punish you. They are God's servants, sent for the very purpose of punishing those who do what is wrong.*

- **14:9**—*Christ died and rose again for this very purpose—to be Lord both of the living and of the dead.*

Pure Genius. (Factoid: Average IQ ranges from 90-110; genius is rated above 140.) Bobby Fischer, an American chess Grandmaster with an IQ of 187, learned the moves of a chess game at age 6. He dropped out of high school at 16 to devote himself fully to his passion. He died in 2008. Johann Wolfgang von Goethe, a German poet and writer, is said to have had an IQ of 210. At the early age of 8, he'd already acquired some knowledge of Greek, Latin, French, and Italian. He died in 1832. How great to serve an eternal and everlasting God who has an IQ that's infinitely incalculable. To get a glimpse of the extreme degree of the unfathomable genius of our God, you only need to consider your Master's unique, loving plan for you, a plan designed before the earth was formed.

1 CORINTHIANS

Wisdom of God. *²⁴But to those called by God to salvation, both Jews and Gentiles, Christ is the power of God and the wisdom of God. ²⁵This foolish plan of God is wiser than the wisest of human plans, and God's weakness is stronger than the greatest of human strength. ²⁶Remember, dear brothers and sisters, that few of you were wise in the world's eyes or powerful or wealthy when God called you (1 Corinthians 1:24-26).*

- **Life Purpose App: Remember that God's call to salvation in Christ has nothing to do with earthly possessions or titles.**

Paul's Message of Wisdom. *¹When I first came to you, dear brothers and sisters, I didn't use lofty words and impressive wisdom to tell you God's secret plan. ...⁷No, the wisdom we speak of is the mystery of God—his plan that was previously hidden, even though he made it for our ultimate glory before the world began. ...¹⁰But it was to us that God revealed these things by his Spirit. For his Spirit searches out everything and shows us God's deep secrets. ¹¹No one can know a person's thoughts except that person's own spirit, and no one can know God's thoughts except God's own Spirit. ¹²And we have received God's Spirit (not the world's spirit), so we can know the wonderful things God has freely given us. ...¹⁶For, "Who can know the Lord's thoughts? Who knows enough* to teach him?" *But we understand these things, for we have the mind of Christ (1 Corinthians 2:1, 7, 10-12, 16).*

- **Life Purpose App: Through Holy Spirit revelation, you have the mind of Christ and understand God's deep secrets, wisdom, mystery, and plan of salvation through Jesus.**

The Lord Assigns Work. *⁵Each of us [Apollos and Paul] did the work the Lord gave us. ⁶I planted the seed in your hearts, and Apollos watered it, but it was God who made it grow. ⁷It's not important who does the planting, or who does the watering. What's important is that God makes the seed grow. ⁸The one who plants and the one who waters work together with the same purpose. And both will be rewarded for their own hard work (Romans 3:5-8).*

- **Life Purpose App: Do the purposeful work God gives you, and you'll be rewarded.**

Judgment Day. *¹³But on the judgment day, fire will reveal what kind of work each builder has done. The fire will show if a person's work has any value. ¹⁴If the work survives, that builder will receive a reward. ¹⁵But if the work is burned up, the builder will suffer great loss. The builder will be saved, but like someone barely escaping through a wall of flames (1 Corinthians 3:13-15).*

- **Life Purpose App: If your work has value, you'll be rewarded.**

Shadowboxing. *²⁴Don't you realize that in a race everyone runs, but only one person gets the prize? So run to win! ²⁵All athletes are disciplined in their training. They do it to win a prize that will fade away, but we do it for an eternal prize. ²⁶So I run with purpose in every step. I am not just shadowboxing. ²⁷I discipline my body like an athlete, training it to do what it should. Otherwise, I fear that after preaching to others I myself might be disqualified (1 Corinthians 9:24-27).*

- **Life Purpose App: Run with purpose in every step to win an eternal prize.**

Spiritual Gifts. *⁶God works in different ways, but it is the same God who does the work in all of us. ⁷A spiritual gift is given to each of us so we can help each other (1 Corinthians 12:6-7).*

- **Life Purpose App: Use your spiritual gifts to help others.**

SUMMARY QUESTIONS FOR 1 CORINTHIANS: What do these six practical applications suggest as your next step toward God's impeccable plan for you? Will you take that step?

- Remember that God's call to salvation in Christ has nothing to do with earthly possessions or titles.

- Through Holy Spirit revelation, you have the mind of Christ and understand God's deep secrets, wisdom, mystery, and plan of salvation through Jesus.

- Do the purposeful work God gives you, and you'll be rewarded.

- If your work has value, you'll be rewarded.

- Run with purpose in every step to win an eternal prize.

- Use your spiritual gifts to help others.

2 CORINTHIANS

Our Heavenly Dwelling. *¹For we know that when this earthly tent we live in is taken down (that is, when we die and leave this earthly body), we will have a house in heaven, an eternal body made for us by God himself and not by human hands. ...⁵God himself has prepared us for this, and as a guarantee he has given us his Holy Spirit (2 Corinthians 5:1, 5).*

- **Life Purpose App: Our purpose is to live in heaven eternally with God.** You were created to live forever with God in heaven. In the meantime, while you await your eternal home, you have the Holy Spirit to direct your steps on earth. In what way do you rely on the Holy Spirit to guide you into the future reserved for you?

Christ's Representatives. *God has given us the task of telling everyone what he is doing. We're Christ's representatives. God uses us to persuade men and women to drop their differences and enter into God's work of making things right between them. We're speaking for Christ himself now: Become friends with God; he's already a friend with you (2 Corinthians 5:18-20 The Message).*

- **Life Purpose App: Our purpose is to be Christ's messenger.** What a privilege to deliver this message of hope to people from Jesus: *"Become friends with God; he's already a friend with you."* What's your favorite way of saying this—in your own words? Will this be a message you can deliver to the world?

What's Your Message To the World? If you were a marketing vice president for Coca-Cola®, you'd have been greatly rewarded for helping create the buzz and message for Coca-Cola Zero®: *"Real Coke Taste. Zero Calories."* The 2006 product launch for this soda has been one of the most successful campaigns in the history of the company, recently selling more than 600 million cases globally in one year.[9] So, what's your message to the world and what eternal reward do you think you'll receive in heaven for creating a buzz about Jesus?

GALATIANS

Paul's Mission: To proclaim the good news about Jesus to the Gentiles—those who were not Jewish.

Background: The book of Galatians is all about the gift of grace. It's about freedom from thinking that you have to be a slave to rules and legalism to earn God's approval. Paul wanted people to know that God had set them free from the Old Law—that this is the good news of the gospel that had been revealed to him.

- **Paul's Message Comes From Christ.** *¹³You know what I [Paul] was like when I followed the Jewish religion—how I violently persecuted God's church. I did my best to destroy it. ¹⁴I was far ahead of my fellow Jews in my zeal for the traditions of my ancestors. ¹⁵But even before I was born, God chose me and called me by his marvelous grace. Then it pleased him ¹⁶to reveal his Son to me so that I would proclaim the Good News about Jesus to the Gentiles (Galatians 1:13-16).*

Reflection Questions:

1. How do you feel about being rescued by Jesus' grace to freely and gratefully follow the exceptionally detailed plan laid out for your life—versus being obliged by laws, rules, duty, fear, and guilt to obey God?

2. With abundant grace, God chose and called Paul, a sinner, before he was even born, to reveal good news to a hurting world. With abundant grace showered on you, too, what dynamic and exciting assignment do you feel God may have put in your heart before you were even born?

Prayer: God, your grace is not only sufficient, it's the greatest gift ever—the best news of a lifetime! Thank you that your grace enables me to accomplish all you've arranged for me to do on earth.

MULLING THINGS OVER

(Draw a picture, write a song, journal your thoughts, or tape in a photo or other keepsake related to your life purpose. Or you can do a *brain dump* list of the things causing your mind to wander—as you pray for God to reveal your boldest life purpose.)

EPHESIANS

God's Plan. *Furthermore, because we are united with Christ, we have received an inheritance from God, for he chose us in advance, and he makes everything work out according to his plan (Ephesians 1:11).*

- **Life Purpose App: God, who chose you, makes everything work out on purpose.**

God's Masterpiece. *For we are God's masterpiece. He has created us anew in Christ Jesus, so we can do the good things he planned for us long ago (Ephesians 2:10).*

- **Life Purpose App: You're God's masterpiece, made new in Christ to do the good things planned long ago for you to do.**

God's Mysterious Plan Revealed. *⁶And this is God's plan: Both Gentiles and Jews who believe the Good News share equally in the riches inherited by God's children. Both are part of the same body, and both enjoy the promise of blessings because they belong to Christ Jesus. ...⁹I [Paul] was chosen to explain to everyone this mysterious plan that God, the Creator of all things, had kept secret from the beginning. ¹⁰God's purpose in all this was to use the church to display his wisdom in its rich variety to all the unseen rulers and authorities in the heavenly places.*

[11]*This was his eternal plan, which he carried out through Christ Jesus our Lord (Ephesians 3:6, 9-11).*

- **Life Purpose App: God's wise plan for you is salvation through faith in Christ Jesus and a place for you in the church, which is the body of Christ.**

Extra info as you ponder this important passage: It was God's perfectly wise, loving, and secret plan/purpose (from the very beginning) that Jesus would be the Savior of the Gentiles, too, not just the Jews; that all these Christ-followers would be united in one body, one family, the church; and that all would share equally in the riches inherited by God's children. But why was the plan to be kept secret? So that God's magnificently diverse wisdom would astonish all of heaven with the revelation of this stunning plan to redeem the world after the fall!

God's Mighty Power. *Now all glory to God, who is able, through his mighty power at work within us, to accomplish infinitely more than we might ask or think (Ephesians 3:20).*

- **Life Purpose App: You're able to accomplish infinitely more than you might ask or think because of the mighty power of God.**

God's Call. *Therefore I [Paul], a prisoner for serving the Lord, beg you to lead a life worthy of your calling, for you have been called by God (Ephesians 4:1).*

- **Life Purpose App: Lead a life worthy of God's calling.**

God's Will. *Don't act thoughtlessly, but understand what the Lord wants you to do (Ephesians 5:17).*

- **Life Purpose App: Understand what's expected of you.**

SUMMARY QUESTIONS FOR EPHESIANS: What do these six practical applications suggest as a next step to help you discover and fulfill God's glorious plan for your life? Will you take that step?

- God, who chose you, makes everything work out on purpose.

- You're God's masterpiece, made new in Christ to do the good things planned long ago for you to do.

- God's wise plan for you is salvation through faith in Christ Jesus and a place for you in the church, which is the body of Christ.

- You're able to accomplish infinitely more than you might ask or think because of the mighty power of God.

- Lead a life worthy of God's calling.

- Understand what's expected of you.

PHILIPPIANS

God's Good Work in You. *And I [Paul] am certain that God, who began the good work within you, will continue his work until it is finally finished on the day when Christ Jesus returns (Philippians 1:6).*

- **Life Purpose App: God began and will complete a good work in you.** God didn't put you on earth without a strategic plan for your life—that includes character building and good deeds done in the name of Christ. In what way is it encouraging to know that you only need to cooperate with God, not create your own character transformation or brilliant life plan?

One Mind and Purpose. *Then make me [Paul] truly happy by agreeing wholeheartedly with each other, loving one another, and working together with one mind and purpose (Philippians 2:2).*

- **Life Purpose App: God's purpose is for you to think like Christ.** God wants you to love others and work well with them by sharing the mind and purposes of Christ. In what situation (at home, at school, at work, during athletics, during hobbies) have you found yourself involved with someone who wasn't of the mind of Christ or wasn't filled with the purpose of knowing Christ? Did or does that make it difficult for you to get to know Christ more intimately or move forward with your wildly significant life purpose?

Jesus Died in Humble Obedience. *He [Jesus] humbled himself in obedience to God and died a criminal's death on a cross (Philippians 2:8).*

- **Life Purpose App: God's plan requires humble obedience.** Humility is a foundational character trait on which every other trait rests. For example, you can't be generous if you're not humble. You can't be patient if you're not humble. You can't be self-controlled or content or encouraging, among many other things, if you're not humble. Jesus, innocent of all charges, was humble to the point of submitting to death on the cross to ensure your eternal life. What step can you take toward humility that would bless God, you, others, and your life mission?

We'd all like to be humble. But what if nobody notices?

—John Ortberg, pastor and author

COLOSSIANS

Knowledge of God's Will. *⁹We ask God to give you complete knowledge of his will and to give you spiritual wisdom and understanding. ¹⁰Then the way you live will always honor and please the Lord, and your lives will produce every kind of good fruit. All the while, you will grow as you learn to know God better and better. ¹¹We also pray that you will be strengthened with all his glorious power so you will have all the endurance and patience you need (Colossians 1:9-11).*

- **Life Purpose App: Pray for complete knowledge of God's will, spiritual wisdom and understanding, and the strength of God's glorious power.**

God's Mysterious Plan Is Christ Himself. *²I want them [Christians] to have complete confidence that they understand God's mysterious plan, which is Christ himself. ³In him lie hidden all the treasures of wisdom and knowledge (Colossians 2:2-3).*

- **Life Purpose App: Pray for a confident understanding of God's mysterious plan, which is faith in Christ.**

God's Mysterious Plan Concerning Christ. *Pray for us, too, that God will give us many opportunities to speak about his mysterious plan concerning Christ. That is why I am here in chains (Colossians 4:3).*

- **Life Purpose App: Pray for opportunities to speak out about God's mysterious plan, which is Christ's saving grace.**

Extra Insight on God's Mysterious Plan About Christ. This passage from Ephesians sheds light on our verses from Colossians by explaining that surrendering to Christ is the plan!

⁹God has now revealed to us his mysterious plan regarding Christ, a plan to fulfill his own good pleasure. ¹⁰And this is the plan: At the right time he will bring everything together under the authority of Christ—everything in heaven and on earth (Ephesians 1:9-10).

SUMMARY QUESTIONS FOR COLOSSIANS: So, the mysterious plan of God, which the Bible and Holy Spirit help you understand, is the gracious plan of salvation by faith in Christ Jesus. Since this is God's immeasurably wise plan for all people, your life purpose is to:

- Pray for complete knowledge of God's will, spiritual wisdom and understanding, and the strength of God's glorious power.

- Pray for a confident understanding of God's mysterious plan, which is faith in Christ.

- Pray for opportunities to speak out about God's mysterious plan, which is Christ's saving grace.

What unique role do you think God may be asking you to play in this worldwide, eternal plan? Will you step into that role now?

The wise still seek him.

—Author unknown

1 THESSALONIANS

Don't Be a People-Pleaser. *For we speak as messengers approved by God to be entrusted with the Good News. Our purpose is to please God, not people. He alone examines the motives of our hearts (1 Thessalonians 2:4).*

- **Life Purpose App: Your purpose is to please God, not people.** Paul was writing to the Christians in the Greek city of Thessalonica about his team (Timothy, Silas, and himself), explaining their purpose in preaching the gospel: to please God alone. Which people do you try to please, and why? In what way might that change completely or grow weaker or stronger as your long-term life purpose unfolds?

Live to Please God. *¹Finally, dear brothers and sisters, we urge you in the name of the Lord Jesus to live in a way that pleases God, as we have taught you. ...³God's will is for you to be holy, so stay away from all sexual sin. ⁴Then each of you will control his own body and live in holiness and honor—⁵not in lustful*

128

passion like the pagans who do not know God and his ways. ...⁷God has called us to live holy lives, not impure lives (1 Thessalonians 4:1, 3-5, 7).

- **Life Purpose App: God calls you to live a holy life of purity.** To please God and be holy, you're to stay away from all sexual sin. Paul is clear that living in holiness means controlling your body and not giving in to lustful passion like people who don't know God. In what way do you think purity impacts your primary, far-reaching assignment for God?

Paul's Final Advice. *¹⁶Always be joyful. ¹⁷Never stop praying. ¹⁸Be thankful in all circumstances, for this is God's will for you who belong to Christ Jesus. ¹⁹Do not stifle the Holy Spirit (1 Thessalonians 5:16-19).*

- **Life Purpose App: God's will for you is to be joyful, prayerful, thankful, and in tune with the Holy Spirit.** How is it easy or hard for you to follow Paul's advice about this attitude? Imagine attempting to complete the unique task God has assigned you without being grateful for the assignment—or joyful, or in tune with the Holy Spirit! Would that make you bitter, angry, jealous, or lazy? What words would describe you if you tried pursuing God's incredible mission for your life without the right attitude?

The best things are nearest: breath in your nostrils, light in your eyes, flowers at your feet, duties at your hand, the path of God just before you.

—Robert Louis Stevenson, Scottish novelist and poet

2 THESSALONIANS

Encouragement for Christians. *So we keep on praying for you, asking our God to enable you to live a life worthy of his call. May he give you the power to accomplish all the good things your faith prompts you to do (2 Thessalonians 1:11).*

- This verse makes two points:

  - Live a life worthy of God's call.

  - Accomplish all the good things your faith prompts you to do.

Christians Should Stand Firm. *¹⁴He [God] called you to salvation when we told you the Good News; now you can share in the glory of our Lord Jesus Christ. ¹⁵With all these things in mind, dear brothers and sisters, stand firm and keep a strong grip on the teaching we passed on to you both in person and by letter. ¹⁶Now may our Lord Jesus Christ himself and God our Father, who loved us and by his grace gave us eternal comfort and a wonderful hope, ¹⁷comfort you and strengthen you in every good thing you do and say (2 Thessalonians 2:14-17).*

- This passage makes two similar points:

  - God called you to salvation.

  - May you be comforted and strengthened in every good thing you do and say.

- **Life Purpose App for Both Passages: Now that God has called you, do and say good things.**

SUMMARY QUESTIONS FOR 2 THESSALONIANS: How do these two passages point you in the direction of your God-inspired legacy? Will you take a step now toward it?

MULLING THINGS OVER

(Draw a picture, write a song, journal your thoughts, or tape in a photo or other keepsake related to your life purpose. Or you can do a *brain dump* list of the things causing your mind to wander—as you pray for God to reveal your boldest life purpose.)

1 TIMOTHY

Paul's Gratitude for God's Mercy. *¹²I thank Christ Jesus our Lord, who has given me strength to do his work. He considered me trustworthy and appointed me to serve him, ¹³even though I used to blaspheme the name of Christ. In my insolence, I persecuted his people. But God had mercy on me because I did it in ignorance and unbelief. ¹⁴Oh, how generous and gracious our Lord was! He filled me with the faith and love that come from Christ Jesus (1 Timothy 1:12-14).*

- **Life Purpose App: Thank God for the principle of "Even Though"— in relation to being appointed to serve.** One of the greatest mysteries of all times is why God would use us to do kingdom work, even though we're sinners! Paul states it best when he says that even though he used to curse the name of Christ, God still appointed him. Even though Paul was insolent (disrespectful), God generously and graciously had mercy on him. How do you feel about this unusual principle that allows you to be on-mission for God in a big way, even though you are a sinner? (Not that the principle filled with grace and mercy condones sinning, of course!)

A Good Servant of Christ Jesus. *"Physical training is good, but training for godliness is much better, promising benefits in this life and in the life to come"* *(1 Timothy 4:8).*

- **Life Purpose App: Get the training you need to become more like Christ.** You may be a top-notch athlete or you may prefer to boycott all things exercise! Regardless, you can't dispute the lasting benefits of a good physical workout. But how are you doing with your *spiritual* training these days? Have you been strengthening those muscles, or have you turned into a Christian couch potato? Who could coach, mentor, or disciple you to be all God wants you to be?

Impossible Tasks. So, you may be able to wiggle your ears, touch your tongue to your nose, or lick your elbow. But have you ever tried to look at your eyebrows without a mirror or make a sand rope or tickle yourself to the point of laughter? Those three tasks are humanly impossible. Also impossible for you are these three actions:

- Being your own Savior.

- Restoring yourself daily from sin.

- Creating a significant purpose for your life.

Only God can do those things!

2 TIMOTHY

Encouragement to Be Faithful. *For God saved us and called us to live a holy life. He did this, not because we deserved it, but because that was his plan from before the beginning of time—to show us his grace through Christ Jesus (2 Timothy 1:9).*

- **Life Purpose App: God calls you, by grace, to live a holy life.**

An Approved Worker. *[20]In a wealthy home some utensils are made of gold and silver, and some are made of wood and clay. The expensive utensils are used for special occasions, and the cheap ones are for everyday use. [21]If you keep yourself pure, you will be a special utensil for honorable use. Your life will be clean, and you will be ready for the Master to use you for every good work (2 Timothy 2:20-21).*

- **Life Purpose App: Keep yourself pure so you'll be ready for the Master to use you for every good work.**

The Wisdom of Scripture. *[16]All Scripture is inspired by God and is useful to teach us what is true and to make us realize what is wrong in our lives. It corrects us when we are wrong and teaches us to do what is right. [17]God uses it to prepare and equip his people to do every good work (2 Timothy 3:16-17).*

- **Life Purpose App: God's purpose for Scripture is to teach, convict, correct, prepare, and equip you to do every good work.**

Offer Your Life to God. *But you should keep a clear mind in every situation. Don't be afraid of suffering for the Lord. Work at telling others the Good News, and fully carry out the ministry God has given you (2 Timothy 4:5).*

- **Life Purpose App: Share the gospel and fully carry out the ministry God has given you.**

SUMMARY QUESTIONS FOR 2 TIMOTHY: What do these four practical applications suggest as a next step toward God's most enthralling purpose for you? Will you take that step?

- God calls you, by grace, to live a holy life.

- Keep yourself pure so you'll be ready for the Master to use you for every good work.

- God's purpose for Scripture is to teach, convict, correct, prepare, and equip you to do every good work.

- Share the gospel and fully carry out the ministry God has given you.

TITUS

Paul's Assignment. *¹I [Paul] have been sent to proclaim faith to those God has chosen and to teach them to know the truth that shows them how to live godly lives. ...³It is by the command of God our Savior that I have been entrusted with this work for him (Titus 1:1, 3).*

- **Life Purpose App: God entrusts you with important kingdom-building work.** Paul was not only passionate about teaching truths that had practical application for people's lives, but he was also passionate about obeying whatever God commanded him to do. In what way does learning to obey God's commands on a daily basis prepare you well to complete the important life work with which you've been entrusted?

Filling a Need. Did you know that the first tin cans were so thick they had to be hammered open with the help of a chisel? As cans became thinner, William Lyman was inspired in 1870 to invent the first familiar household can opener, the rotary kind you hand crank. Lyman's device used a rotating wheel and a sharp edge versus today's saw-toothed wheel. And his can opener first had to pierce the center of the can.[10] If Lyman hadn't filled this need in households, do you think somebody else would have come along eventually to do it? Yes, of course—even though that person may have had a different vision of what the end product would look like! Likewise, if Paul hadn't obeyed the command of God, our Savior, to do the work entrusted to him, somebody else would have been given his task—even though that person's approach would have been unique.

PHILEMON

Paul's Thanksgiving. *⁴I [Paul] always thank my God when I pray for you, Philemon, ⁵because I keep hearing about your faith in the Lord Jesus and your love for all of God's people (Philemon 1:4-5).*

- **Life Purpose App: Grow your faith in Jesus and your love for people to prepare yourself to live the life you're meant to live.** Paul's letter includes a request that Philemon welcome back his slave (Onesimus) as a brother in Christ, not as a slave. Paul is applauding Philemon for his love of all God's people, a love overflowing with faith that grasps the enormity of Christ's goodness. In what way is your faith increasing your love for those outside your social circle and/or for those you know God has destined you to serve in a specific way?

Bunch of Grapes Auctioned for $910 in Japan. On August 11, 2008, msnbc.com reported that a new variety of premium Ruby Roman grapes debuted in a Japanese auction and sold for a record-high price of 100,000 yen (about $910) per bunch. And other reports confirm that a hotel manager did, indeed, pay about $26 for each ping-pong-size grape. It's generally known that fruit is expensive in Japan and that people often buy high-end grapes, peaches, and melons as luxury gifts, but that's a whole lot of yen! In light of that, how would you describe the value of your faith? What about the value of your three most treasured relationships? Priceless?

MULLING THINGS OVER

(Draw a picture, write a song, journal your thoughts, or tape in a photo or other keepsake related to your life purpose. Or you can do a *brain dump* list of the things causing your mind to wander—as you pray for God to reveal your boldest life purpose.)

HEBREWS

The Purpose of Hebrews' Chapter 11: To highlight for us the purpose-filled heroes in God's Hall of Great Faith.

Background: Hebrews 11 carefully recounts the names and faith experiences of Old Testament men and women who firmly believed in God's promises and persevered to do the Lord's will despite dangers and fears. Here's a slice of the chapter that reflects the enormous faith of some of the purposeful people who lived faithful lives. (If you've not recently read all of Chapter 11, put it on your reading list!)

- **Heroes of the Bible:** *32How much more do I need to say? It would take too long to recount the stories of the faith of Gideon, Barak, Samson, Jephthah, David, Samuel, and all the prophets. 33By faith these people overthrew kingdoms, ruled with justice, and received what God had promised them. They shut the mouths of lions, 34quenched the flames of fire, and escaped death by the edge of the sword. Their weakness was turned to strength. They became strong in battle and put whole armies to flight. 35Women received their loved ones back again from death. But others were tortured, refusing to turn from God in order to be set free. They placed their hope in a better life after the resurrection.*

³⁶Some were jeered at, and their backs were cut open with whips. Others were chained in prisons. ³⁷Some died by stoning, some were sawed in half, and others were killed with the sword. Some went about wearing skins of sheep and goats, destitute and oppressed and mistreated (Hebrews 11:32-37).

Reflection Questions:

1. Of all the tasks and challenges listed in verses 33-37, which one do you relate to the most or which one inspires you to be as purposeful as possible, and why?

2. When your name gets written on God's list of "Purpose-Filled, Great Faith Heroes," what 10 words would you like to describe your extraordinary, daring adventure for the Lord?

Prayer: God, give me a sacrificial faith that pleases you. Give me an obedient faith in spite of setbacks in fulfilling my life purpose. And give me a fearless faith that invites miracles.

ANOTHER GREAT PURPOSE VERSE IN HEBREWS:

- **12:1**—*Therefore, since we are surrounded by such a huge crowd of witnesses to the life of faith, let us strip off every weight that slows us down, especially the sin that so easily trips us up. And let us run with endurance the race God has set before us.*

JAMES

Faith Without Good Deeds is Useless. *14What good is it, dear brothers and sisters, if you say you have faith but don't show it by your actions? Can that kind of faith save anyone? 15Suppose you see a brother or sister who has no food or clothing, 16and you say, "Good-bye and have a good day; stay warm and eat well"—but then you don't give that person any food or clothing. What good does that do? 17So you see, faith by itself isn't enough. Unless it produces good deeds, it is dead and useless. 18Now someone may argue, "Some people have faith; others have good deeds." But I say, "How can you show me your faith if you don't have good deeds? I will show you my faith by my good deeds." 19You say you have faith, for you believe that there is one God. Good for you! Even the demons believe this, and they tremble in terror. 20How foolish! Can't you see that faith without good deeds is useless? (James 2:14-20).*

- **Life Purpose App: Show your faith by good deeds.** James explains that faith in God is one-half of the important equation of life and that letting your faith spill into action is the other half. To which side might your life be more weighted, and why? Will any imbalance sabotage your effectiveness when you get deep into fulfilling your heart's desire—deep into the heart of your life mission?

Warning about Self-Confidence. *¹³Look here, you who say, "Today or tomorrow we are going to a certain town and will stay there a year. We will do business there and make a profit." ¹⁴How do you know what your life will be like tomorrow? Your life is like the morning fog—it's here a little while, then it's gone. ¹⁵What you ought to say is, "If the Lord wants us to, we will live and do this or that." ¹⁶Otherwise you are boasting about your own plans, and all such boasting is evil. ¹⁷Remember, it is sin to know what you ought to do and then not do it (James 4:13-17).*

- **Life Purpose App: Follow God's plan—and only God's plan.** When discovering your life purpose, be careful not to run ahead of God or lag behind. Staying in God's will with just the right amount of self-confidence and God-confidence is actually an art, not an exact science. A timeless guideline is this: *When there's confusion, wait!* Be careful, though, not to catch the deadly "disease" called Analysis Paralysis—meaning you stand frozen in fear, paralyzed and overanalyzing every single detail, not wanting to act without God's clear direction and blessing. If you find yourself trapped in that type of fear, it's best to calm yourself by breathing deeply into a paper bag to prevent hyperventilation—and then go ahead and take a baby step. Just do some type of low-cost inquiry in the direction you suspect you're being asked to go. God can close a door, as needed. What's been your experience with being overly confident about your plans versus being paralyzed by analyzing too many options for too long? Can you strike a happy medium—a balance that will serve your lifetime dream well?

Analysis Paralysis Is a Critical Problem. In sports, an athlete may think too much about what to do next, become mentally paralyzed, and fail to react in enough time to make a strategic play! In board games, analysis paralysis happens when a player becomes overwhelmed by how one move will affect another move later in the game. In chess, for example, it's so prevalent, that it's even been named The Kotov Syndrome (from Alexander Kotov's 1971 book, *Think Like a Grandmaster*), which means a player thinks very hard for a long time, doesn't find a clear path, runs low on time, and makes a poor move at the last second.

MULLING THINGS OVER

(Draw a picture, write a song, journal your thoughts, or tape in a photo or other keepsake related to your life purpose. Or you can do a *brain dump* list of the things causing your mind to wander—as you pray for God to reveal your boldest life purpose.)

1 PETER

Royal Priesthood. *But you are not like that, for you are a chosen people. You are royal priests, a holy nation, God's very own possession. As a result, you can show others the goodness of God, for he called you out of the darkness into his wonderful light (1 Peter 2:9).*

- **Life Purpose App: You're a royal priest, set apart for a holy purpose to show God's goodness.**

    - **You're a royal priest.** That is...one who offers sacrifices to God. In what way will you offer your life as a living sacrifice?

    - **You're a holy nation.** That is...a member of Christ's church consecrated to God. In what way do you help members of the body of Christ to be holy by your example of holiness?

- **You're God's very own possession.** That is...a tool in the Master's hand. How have you been usable in the past? In what way are you willing to be usable to the highest degree possible in the future?

- **You're expected to show others the goodness of God.** What is your favorite way of "showing off" God and pointing people toward him?

- **You've been called out of the darkness into God's wonderful light.** How do you show your gratitude for this calling?

Live for God. *⁷The end of the world is coming soon. Therefore, be earnest and disciplined in your prayers. ⁸Most important of all, continue to show deep love for each other, for love covers a multitude of sins. ⁹Cheerfully share your home with those who need a meal or a place to stay. ¹⁰God has given each of you a gift from his great variety of spiritual gifts. Use them well to serve one another. ¹¹Do you have the gift of speaking? Then speak as though God himself were speaking through you. Do you have the gift of helping others? Do it with all the strength and energy that God supplies. Then everything you do will bring glory to God through Jesus Christ (1 Peter 4:7-11).*

- **Life Purpose App: Pray, love, share, and use your spiritual gifts to serve others—and do all this with the strength and energy that God supplies.** Peter spells out exactly what's needed for living a life that brings glory to God. In what way is each of these Christian practices a thorough training ground for your often-intense mission in life?

  - Pray earnest and disciplined prayers.

  - Show deep love for one another.

  - Cheerfully share your home.

  - Use your spiritual gifts to serve one another.

2 PETER

Growing in Faith. *³By his divine power, God has given us everything we need for living a godly life. ...⁵In view of all this, make every effort to respond to God's promises. Supplement your faith with a generous provision of moral excellence, and moral excellence with knowledge, ⁶and knowledge with self-control, and self-control with patient endurance, and patient endurance with godliness, ⁷and godliness with brotherly affection, and brotherly affection with love for everyone. ⁸The more you grow like this, the more productive and useful you will be in your knowledge of our Lord Jesus Christ (2 Peter 1:3, 5-8).*

- **Life Purpose App: The purpose of growing in your faith is to prepare yourself better to share Christ.** Peter encourages moral excellence, knowledge, self-control, patient endurance, godliness, and brotherly affection with love. By growing spiritually in this way, you gain a deeper knowledge of Christ who guides your walk, enlarges your heart, and makes you holy. In this process, you learn to surrender to the will of God, and you become more productive and useful. What immediate step can you take to supplement your faith and be more productive in the work you were put on earth to do?

You're the Creation of the Incomparable God. Leonardo da Vinci worked diligently for four years on his monumental composition, an oil painting of Mona Lisa. Michelangelo painted the ceiling of the Sistine Chapel (standing on scaffolds with a painful crick in his neck) for four years. Ten different contractors and their subcontractors spent four years constructing the Golden Gate Bridge. How long did it take God to design you? It was effortless and single-handedly, eons ago before the world began; in the flash of a God moment. (That's like less than a zillionth of the time it takes you to blink!)

MULLING THINGS OVER

(Draw a picture, write a song, journal your thoughts, or tape in a photo or other keepsake related to your life purpose. Or you can do a *brain dump* list of the things causing your mind to wander—as you pray for God to reveal your boldest life purpose.)

Have patience with all things, but chiefly have patience with yourself. Do not lose courage in considering your own imperfections, but instantly set about remedying them—every day begin the task anew.

—Francis de Sales, bishop of Geneva, 1567-1622

1 JOHN
2 JOHN
3 JOHN

On-the-go-with 1 John...

Please God and Live Forever. *¹⁵Do not love this world nor the things it offers you, for when you love the world, you do not have the love of the Father in you. ¹⁶For the world offers only a craving for physical pleasure, a craving for everything we see, and pride in our achievements and possessions. These are not from the Father, but are from this world. ¹⁷And this world is fading away, along with everything that people crave. But anyone who does what pleases God will live forever (1 John 2:15-17).*

- **Life Purpose App: Don't love this world.** From chocolate to alcohol, from fame to fortune, from clothes to cars—you're constantly bombarded with cravings in this world. The temptations are endless for things that will bring pleasure. In what way might your biggest craving, most prideful achievement, or most ego-based possession distract you and keep you focused on the things of this earth, rather than on the eternal impact you're destined to have?

On-the-go with 2 John...

God's Command. *⁵I [John] am writing to remind you, dear friends, that we should love one another. This is not a new commandment, but one we have had from the beginning. ⁶Love means doing what God has commanded us, and he has commanded us to love one another, just as you heard from the beginning (2 John 1:5-6).*

- **Life Purpose App: Love one another.** John's words echo from the story in Matthew 22 when Jesus was asked to name the most important commandment. The crowd heard a startling answer: Love! Love the Lord your God with all your heart, soul, and mind—and love your neighbor as yourself. Why do you think love is such a foundational purpose in life, especially in light of your "This I Must Do" mission?

On-the-go with 3 John...

God's Children. *Follow only what is good. Remember that those who do good prove that they are God's children, and those who do evil prove that they do not know God (3 John 1:11).*

- **Life Purpose App: Do what's good and prove that you're God's child.** Doing Good=God and Doing Evil=devil. In what way have you recently done what's good and proved that you're a child of God, even when the world screamed at you to do evil? How many devils does it take to destroy a world-class ministry? One!

Watch to see where God is at work and join him!

—Henry Blackaby and Claude King, authors of *Experiencing God*

JUDE

A Call to Remain Faithful. *[17]But you, my dear friends, must remember what the apostles of our Lord Jesus Christ said. [18]They told you that in the last times there would be scoffers whose purpose in life is to satisfy their ungodly desires. [19]These people are the ones who are creating divisions among you. They follow their natural instincts because they do not have God's Spirit in them. [20]But you, dear friends, must build each other up in your most holy faith, pray in the power of the Holy Spirit, [21]and await the mercy of our Lord Jesus Christ, who will bring you eternal life. In this way, you will keep yourselves safe in God's love. [22]And you must show mercy to those whose faith is wavering. [23]Rescue others by snatching them from the flames of judgment. Show mercy to still others, but do so with great caution, hating the sins that contaminate their lives (Jude 1:17-23).*

- **Life Purpose App: Don't get distracted from God's purposes.** Jude—the probable author of this New Testament book and one of Jesus' half-brothers, who at first didn't believe that Jesus was Lord but later became a missionary—addresses his letter to all who've been called by God. He mentions an unholy scoffer's purpose in life, which is to satisfy the flesh—but he goes on to list many blessed purposes that Christians must have if they want to be counted as faithful:

- Build each other up in your most holy faith

- Pray in the power of the Holy Spirit

- Await the mercy of our Lord Jesus Christ

- Keep yourselves safe in God's love

- Show mercy to those whose faith is wavering

- Rescue others by snatching them from the flames of judgment

- Show mercy to still others

In what way would these Christ-like purposes be an incredible blessing to the Christ-centered contribution you dream of making?

Remain Faithful. The Barbie fashion doll was the idea of an American businesswoman, Ruth Handler, who watched her daughter, Barbara, play with paper dolls as if they were grownups. Barbie has had an *on/off* romantic relationship with her boyfriend, Ken Carson. In 2004, Mattel Inc. announced that Barbie and Ken had decided to split up, but in 2006 the two rekindled their relationship after Ken had a makeover. Despite this, Barbie and Ken are both said to be single at the moment. Ah, the world of dolls and make-believe—such drama! How grateful are you that your great God loves you regardless of how often you pull away to do your own thing, even if that includes pursuing other love interests? The most important question of your life becomes this: Will you remain faithful to God, who has always loved you and will love you into eternity—or will you choose an *on/off* relationship with God?

REVELATION

Vision of the Son of Man. *⁹I, John, am your brother and your partner in suffering and in God's Kingdom and in the patient endurance to which Jesus calls us. I was exiled to the island of Patmos for preaching the word of God and for my testimony about Jesus. ¹⁰It was the Lord's Day, and I was worshiping in the Spirit. Suddenly, I heard behind me a loud voice like a trumpet blast. ¹¹It said, "Write in a book everything you see, and send it to the seven churches in the cities of Ephesus, Smyrna, Pergamum, Thyatira, Sardis, Philadelphia, and Laodicea" (Revelation 1:9-11).*

- **Life Purpose App: Jesus calls you to patient endurance, as you fulfill your clearly outlined purpose in life.** John's calling included, in his later years in exile, writing a book. What are you called to do? How's your patience? Will you endure whatever comes your way, until you can complete the intimidating yet unmistakable task you've been assigned?

Turn From Your Indifference. *[15]"I know all the things you do, that you are neither hot nor cold. I wish that you were one or the other! [16]But since you are like lukewarm water, neither hot nor cold, I will spit [vomit] you out of my mouth! …[19]I correct and discipline everyone I love. So be diligent and turn from your indifference" (Revelation 3:15-16, 19).*

- **Life Purpose App: Jesus will spit you out if your faith is lukewarm.** The church of Laodicea was lukewarm, meaning its members were uncommitted, half-hearted, indecisive, apathetic, and lackadaisical. (See p. 156 for more details about lukewarm water and people.) Out of the seven churches mentioned in Revelation 2–3, this was the only congregation about which the Lord had nothing good to say! It was the wealthiest of these seven churches from Asia Minor (modern-day Turkey) but the most spiritually poor. How are you doing with being red hot—on fire for Jesus and for the *divine urge-dream* you've been called to pursue?

Open the door. *"Look! I stand at the door and knock. If you hear my voice and open the door, I will come in, and we will share a meal together as friends" (Revelation 3:20).*

- **Life Purpose App: Jesus wants to have a personal, eternal relationship with you.** This verse presents an analogy about the messianic banquet with Christ's followers in heaven. It calls to mind a daily Greek habit of sharing of an unhurried, evening meal. That's when family members enjoyed each other's company and exchanged the news of the day. That was much different from their quicker breakfast of a piece of dried bread dipped in wine or shorter lunch break with a picnic snack.

  The image offers a straightforward invitation to get to know Christ. It presents an easy way to open your life to Jesus—to rid yourself of your sense of emptiness and dissatisfaction—and to know for sure that you have a significant purpose. If you long for something more, especially a promise of spending eternity in heaven with Jesus, here are steps 1-2-3!

1. First, realize that Jesus Christ really does want to come into your life.

2. Next, open the door! Salvation won't be forced upon you. It's an invitation you must choose to accept. Do you want to have a personal relationship with Jesus? (See Appendix B if you'd like to read some supporting Scriptures.) If you're ready now, you can open the door by praying a prayer like this:

   Jesus, I believe that you died for me and that God raised you from the dead. Please forgive my sins. You are my Savior. You are my only hope. I want to follow your will for my life. I'm choosing to open the door of my life to you today.

3. Then, Jesus will enter in, dwell with you, dine with you, and be in fellowship with you immediately and forever.

If you haven't yet opened the door for Jesus, would you like to do that now? If so, please tell someone who can rejoice with you. Surely the angels in heaven are rejoicing already!

Endure Persecution. *[12] This means that God's holy people must endure persecution patiently, obeying his commands and maintaining their faith in Jesus. [13] ... "Yes, says the Spirit, they are blessed indeed, for they will rest from their hard work; for their good deeds follow them!" (Revelation 14:12-13).*

- **Life Purpose App: God requires that you maintain your faith in Jesus in spite of persecution.** Nobody likes the thought of being hurt or in pain, but Jesus is saying that God's holy people must endure persecution. And as if that isn't enough, we must do it patiently, obediently, and with a strong faith. What do you think persecution might look like for you at home, in school, locally, or on the worldwide mission field if you follow God's most dramatic plan for your life? Even if you wouldn't be blessed (with rest from your hard work and your good deeds following you) for enduring persecution, as verse 13 promises, what are your thoughts about being persecuted for being a Christian and doing the hard work of that high calling?

Five Lukewarm Facts

To better understand John's entire letter to the church in Laodicea in Revelation 3:14-22, ponder these facts about lukewarm water:

1. Lukewarm water doesn't offer the cleansing or healing power of hot water, nor does it have the refreshing properties of cold water.

2. Physicians used lukewarm water to induce vomiting.

3. Cold and hot drinks were common at feasts, but lukewarm ones weren't favored.

4. The water supply of Laodicea was lukewarm; whereas, nearby Hierapolis had therapeutic hot springs and nearby Colossae had pure, cold, refreshing water. The aqueduct system that probably carried water from the hot mineral springs, allowed the water to become lukewarm and disgusting from a concentration of mineral deposits.[11]

5. Lukewarm is always a compromise of mixing hot with cold. The church at Laodicea was compromising its own doctrinal teaching, allowing it to preach a comfortable, smug, complacent, unchallenging, and religious type of message. Jesus found the church to be nauseating and repulsive and useless—or, to quote 3:17, *"you are wretched and miserable and poor and blind and naked."*

APPENDIX A
THREE LARGE ELEPHANTS IN THE ROOM

I must mention three things about life purpose that you may think are like three large elephants hiding in the room that nobody wants to acknowledge. I wonder if you'd like to talk about these biggies:

- **1st Elephant:** *Can I as a teenager really discover life purpose?*

- **2nd Elephant:** *Won't my life mission morph so much over the years that, later on, the earlier vision will be unrecognizable and useless?*

- **3rd Elephant:** *What if I try really hard to discover my life purpose, but I still can't figure it out? Maybe it's best not to try, rather than face such discouragement.*

These are excellent questions, so let's expose those elephants, one at a time!

1st Elephant: *Can I as a teenager really discover life purpose?*

God has orchestrated a season of life when children goof off, play dodgeball, build forts, ride bikes, enjoy Bible stories, and even learn to do chores and obey their parents. It's intended to be a fairly carefree age of innocence, where they trust their parents to meet all their needs. Those dear children long to hear general concepts from their parents and Sunday school teachers, like these:

- God loves you.

- God is all-powerful.

- God created you special.

- God wants you to tell others about Jesus.

If you're a teenager reading this book, you're ready and eager to hear more specifics. God has a Master Plan for the world to be redeemed, and you're an integral part of that plan. You can accept that you have universal purposes and a unique purpose that are to be carried out in the name of Jesus—seasonally and long-term. You need to hear that God sends all sorts of sneak previews about your life mission and life message—that if you sit still quietly enough to hear God personally call you, you'll receive a revelation about the roles, goals, and lifetime dream that are specifically yours.

And, oh, what a day of rejoicing that is when it all does come together for you! You'll then have somewhere to direct all your young adult passion, as you gather resources, do research, build skill sets, establish a network, attend conferences with experts in your field, grow spiritually, choose a related college major, get an internship and job in your area of passion, and surround yourself with a prayer team—all on purpose for a passionate purpose. You'll be filled with vision that gives you focus and builds your character. You'll be on the pathway to purpose.

Will life get in the way and put up roadblocks every chance it gets? Most definitely! But your passionate ache tucked away in your soul, even during years in a spiritual wilderness or of dealing with a life crisis, will give you hope and a reminder that God loves you enough to have assigned purpose to your life.

Let Jeremiah weigh in about youth

We only need to read Jeremiah 1:7 to know that God's mission for individuals isn't limited by age. According to Bible scholars, Jeremiah was between 14 and 21 years old when God told him: *"Don't say, 'I'm too young,' for you must go wherever I send you and say whatever I tell you."*

In fact, the entire passage (Jeremiah 1:4-12, 17) is so incredible that it deserves to be read to help show that God can make a life mission clear and imminent, regardless of age:

Jeremiah's Call and First Visions. *⁴The Lord gave me this message: ⁵"I knew you before I formed you in your mother's womb. Before you were born I set you apart and appointed you as my prophet to the nations." ⁶"O Sovereign Lord," I said, "I can't speak for you! I'm too young!" ⁷The Lord replied, "Don't say, 'I'm too young,' for you must go wherever I send you and say whatever I tell you. ⁸And don't be afraid of the people, for I will be with you and will protect you. I, the Lord, have spoken!" ⁹Then the Lord reached out and touched my mouth and said, "Look, I have put my words in your mouth! ¹⁰Today I appoint you to stand up against nations and kingdoms. Some you must uproot and tear down, destroy and overthrow. Others you must build up and plant." ¹¹Then the Lord said to me, "Look, Jeremiah! What do you see?" And I replied, "I see a branch from an almond tree." ¹²And the Lord said, "That's right, and it means that I am watching, and I will certainly carry out all my plans." ...¹⁷"Get up and prepare for action. Go out and tell them everything I tell you to say. Do not be afraid of them, or I will make you look foolish in front of them."*

So, yes, God does want teenagers to discover and begin to fulfill their life purpose. For reflection questions on this passage, go to pp. 52-53.

2nd Elephant: *Won't my life mission morph so much over the years that, later on, the earlier vision will be unrecognizable and useless?*

Of course your unique life purpose will morph somewhat as you mature emotionally and spiritually and are better able to understand *God's strategic reasons* for instilling a particular dream. Its core features and passions, though, will remain the same for all time. Would God confuse, frustrate, and play games with us by revealing one vision to us when we're young, only to say later on, "Oops, I changed my mind," and replace it with an all-new vision? No, our God isn't a God of confusion. We're born already fitting into the eternal plan of the Almighty—a plan that was crafted eons ago before the world began. Some have said that the process can feel like watching an old Polaroid photograph appear. It's foggy at first, but soon it's fully developed.

To illustrate this more concretely, let's take a look at one simple clue, out of dozens of clues that can act as a sneak preview from God. This particular clue is reflected in what you think you want to be when you grow up.

What do teenagers want to be when they grow up?

So, what do you want to be when you're older? Does this list help?

Perhaps it's a career in a "Helping" profession:

- Police officer, firefighter, or forest ranger

- Doctor, nurse, veterinarian, or speech therapist

- Teacher, counselor, or social worker

- Priest, nun, pastor, pastor's spouse, or choir director

- Missionary to an impoverished country

- President of your nation/country/company or a politician

- Soldier, military officer, pilot, or railroad conductor

- Scientist, geologist, or inventor

- Attorney or judge

- Author or motivational speaker

- Architect, contractor, builder, or heavy equipment operator

- Professional chef, artist, or musician

- Interior decorator, clothes' designer, or stylist

Perhaps it's a career in an "Exciting" profession:

- Triple threat performer: actor-singer-dancer

- Top-ranked athlete or race car driver

- Somebody famous, like a fashion model, radio broadcaster, or talk show host

- Hobbyist, like a professional surfer, skateboarder, or bicyclist

Nowadays, we can add these popular choices for professions:

- Technological genius

- Environmentalist

- Animal rights' activist

- Reality show star

- Rachel Ray–type of brand icon

What do all these careers have in common? They basically can be divided into two categories: (1) they help someone or some good cause, or (2) they fill a personal need for passion. How can you translate this career clue into usable, long-term, life purpose information? Simply focus on why you want a particular career. Listen to your heart and motive behind the career dream. For example, you may want to be a:

- nurse, who comforts sick people so they aren't afraid.

- firefighter, who helps people escape physical danger.

- dancer, because you love the freedom you feel when you dance.

- ski instructor, so you can be outdoors and teach what you love.

- scientist, because you want to find a cure for cancer to save lives.

- movie star, who's very well paid, famous worldwide, and talented.

- inventor, who gets to create something that makes people's lives better.

- forensic scientist, who takes down the bad guys with crime scene evidence.

How does this relate to life purpose?

God reveals a person's life purpose through, not only career dreams, but also other God-embedded particulars and life circumstances, such as…

- Passions

- Spiritual giftedness

- Talents/skills/abilities

- Hobbies

- Values

- Strengths/weaknesses

- Ministry

- Personality

- Relationships

- Life miracles

- Motives

- Character qualities

- Life experiences

- Opportunities

- Threats/fears

- Prayer life

- Heroes

…among other factors that are fascinating to unpack! So, we can invite a revelation from God by asking a simple question that most people NEVER ask:

"God, how would you like to use me—all of me—in your plan?"

That's the plain and simple formula! God has created you for a purpose. If you're willing to ask that question about how your whole self can be used for God's purposes, you can expect a dependable revelation of your lifelong mission.

Here are some real-life illustrations of how this works in relation to just two factors (career dreams and passions), starting with my own story:

- **Katie**: As a child, I dreamed of being a missionary teacher in Africa and writing a book that gave people hope. I adored Sherlock Holmes mysteries and complicated jigsaw puzzles. Now I'm an author and the founder of a missionary-sending agency that helps people worldwide put together the puzzle of God's plan for their lives. I teach them that God never intended for their life purpose to be a big mystery or puzzle, and that it's possible to simply follow the clues (or put the puzzle pieces together) to invite the revelation.

- **Sally**: As a 27-year-old, she had a girl's dream of being a famous, professional dancer—and also of somehow expanding the peer-mentoring program at her high school to reach more teenagers. Today, she's completed her master's degree and is finishing her clinical hours to become a marriage and family therapist. She volunteers at church in the liturgical dance ministry. Sally daydreams, nearly daily, about opening a Christian camp for teenagers who need counseling and who'd also benefit from dance, music, and art therapy classes that she'd help teach. And, of course, she prays for the camp to become famous worldwide!

- **Drew**: Now 34, he dreamed as a young boy about designing and building tree houses like he had in his backyard. His was a sanctuary for him, a place he could be alone to talk out loud about everything that was on his mind. As a teenager, he became clinically depressed after a drunk driver killed his girlfriend. At age 20, Drew chose to follow Jesus and soon donned a carpenter's tool belt to help his friends build a church. He says, "The hammering helped me get my anger out!" Today, with a powerful faith story of forgiveness, Drew has the privilege of being a men's retreat speaker who takes guys on solitude retreats, where they can get away to talk to God out loud about everything that's on their mind. And he actually has built one very special tree house. He says, "It's not quite as cool as the Swiss Family Robinson house—but my little girl loves it."

Yes, a dream morphs somewhat as a person matures, but we'll always be able to see the threads that weave the tapestry together over the years. It's OK for you to ask for a sneak preview or hint of a revelation regarding your unique mission. Receiving a glimpse of your future, far-reaching assignment will give you something to dream about during the daily-ness of life. God knows that a dream and hope are more valuable than gold when navigating in this fallen world.

So, when you dream of saying, "I want to thank the Academy for this Oscar®," there's no need to discourage yourself from your passionate dream. Instead, remember that it's eternally important to ask, "God, how would you like to use me—all of me—in your plan?"

I guarantee you that your life mission will morph into a more incredible dream than you could ever imagine for yourself, with or without an Oscar®, if you learn to ask God to use you up. You simply can't out-dream God.

3rd Elephant: *What if I try really hard to discover my life purpose, but I still can't figure it out? Maybe it's best not to try, rather than face such discouragement.*

I wish someone had shared with me that *me figuring out* my life mission puts all the pressure on me; whereas, *God revealing* my life mission makes me a recipient of whatever God feels is best for me to know at the time! With that fuller perspective, let's look at the reasons God might choose to withhold information—from a person of any age.

Timing Issues:

- The people God is sending you to serve aren't ready for you—and you're being asked to wait, without any information or explanation. Basically, the delay might not be about you!

- You may be overloaded by some of the current seasonal tasks you've been assigned at home, school, work, church, or in your community— with the critical duties that God has laid out for you in this season of life. Your mission right now simply might be to do your loving best with those responsibilities.

- You may be in crisis right now. You may be facing illness, injury, harm, death of a loved one, unemployment, financial trouble, betrayal, depression, discrimination, and/or recovery challenges—just to mention a few of the ways you may feel like you're dying physically, emotionally, or spiritually. You may be facing intense family dynamics or dire consequences for your actions. You may even be experiencing a loss of faith due to a serious church or ministry upheaval.

Each of these situations requires your undivided attention to heal, which means that your basic life purpose is to move through the Five Stages of Dying. And according to Dr. Elisabeth Kübler-Ross, those stages are Denial, Anger, Bargaining, Depression, and Acceptance. In fact, your purpose is to move forward one small step at a time, so you won't get stuck in those stages. It's even important to move on eventually from the Acceptance stage into an action phase.

Character Issues:

- God may want you, first, to address a character issue like pride, impatience, greed, or self-control that could greatly hinder your life mission. Yes, God called Saul on the Road to Damascus and blinded him to get his attention to do a remarkable 180-degree turnaround, but God's preferred method of launching a life mission is with your cooperation and preparation. You may need to work on issues such as fear, worry, procrastination, distractions, disorganization, or even laziness. Think of this as a gift of time, grace, and character building.

- God may know that you only want the *thrill of the hunt*, which is the thrill of hunting down your life purpose until you capture it—but that you don't really want to do the hard work of the mission itself. Curiosity may be driving you to discover your mission so you'll know what the exciting "IT" is, but God may know that you won't commit to it 100 percent. Let this insight lead you to a crisis of faith that's a life-altering experience. Think of it as the gift of a Motives Do-Over that is priceless.

Faith and Trust Issue:

- God may want you to pray fervently for a long time about your important life mission to increase your faith and trust. This often happens when the mission is so large that to succeed, you'll need to believe—beyond a shadow of doubt—in the power, provision, and protection of God in all you're called to do.

And so, if you're anxiously awaiting God's revelation, allow me to offer these specific words of encouragement to you heart-to-heart:

I know that waiting for your life mission to unfold can been very difficult. And because we really don't know how long you'll have to wait for God to reveal your life direction, it might be helpful if you...

- *Pray, as if you must wait a lifetime for God's plan to be revealed. Prepare your heart and character, as if you'll be launched tomorrow!*

- *In all circumstances, practice patience; it's a virtue that will serve you well forever.*

- *Seek balance in all areas of your life by prioritizing regularly to stay clear about how you want to spend your life.*

- *Take a baby step toward what you do know to be true about your life mission; you can always course-correct if you get a different impression about God's will.*

- *Don't worry. Rest. Be still. Be quiet. Take a break from the intensity of waiting by practicing the art of enjoying God's gift of life.*

I hope the three large elephants have been chased out of the room! God does want to work in your life to unveil the best possible plan at the best possible moment. To cooperate, learn to ask:

God, how would you like to use me—all of me—in your plan?

APPENDIX B
HOW TO MAKE A COMMITMENT TO JESUS

If you think you're ready to make a faith commitment to Jesus, here are a few key biblical truths that can help you make your decision:

Romans 3:23	All have sinned; we all fall short.
Romans 6:23	Heaven is a free gift.
Romans 5:8	Jesus, who loves you, has already paid the penalty for your sins by dying on the cross.
Romans 10:9-10	If you confess that Jesus is Lord, and if you believe that God raised Jesus from the dead, you will be saved.

If you're ready, here's a simple prayer you can say:

Jesus, I believe that you died for me and that God raised you from the dead. Please forgive my sins. You are my Savior. You are my only hope. I want to follow your will for my life.

If you prayed that prayer in faith, please let someone know about your decision, so he or she can encourage you to walk out God's grace-filled, purposeful plan for your life.

If you decided not to say a prayer of confession, I urge you to mark this page and to keep seeking truth with an open heart and mind. And don't be shy about asking to talk with a church leader or Christian friend.

APPENDIX C
HOW TO COOPERATE WITH GOD REGARDING YOUR LIFE PURPOSE

1. If I understand my spiritual gifts, best qualities, and finest values, I'll see undeniable evidence regarding the specific life work God has assigned me.

2. If I rethink my motives, relationships, and use of time, I'm better prepared to answer God's call on my life.

3. If I know myself well—my strengths, weaknesses, opportunities, and threats—God's "This I Must Do" purpose for my life will become clearer and more doable.

4. If I pray for courage, perseverance, and miracles to help me accomplish my life mission, I'll receive those gifts from God.

5. If I accept the unique life purpose that God designed specifically for me, I'll have a bold, passionate lifetime dream that far exceeds my highest hopes.

6. If I surrender my life to Jesus, acknowledging my role as a humble steward of all I've been asked to manage on earth, God will be glorified and I'll be blessed.

APPENDIX D
ENDNOTES

1. www.dictionary.reference.com/browse/googol

2. www.google.com/corporate/history.html

3. www.christianity.about.com/od/oldtestamentbooks/qt/isaiahintro.htm

4. www.animalcorner.co.uk/wildlife/camels/camels_about.html

5. www.eiffel-tower.com

6. www.the-visitor-center.com/pages/Eiffel-Tower/index.htm

7. http://www.taiba.net/awards.php

8. http://www.fcc.gov/cgb/kidszone/history_ans_machine.html

9. www.thecoca-colacompany.com/brands/index.html

10. http://www.lawabel.com/CanOpener_ApoloXII.asp

11. http://www.enjoyinggodministries.com/article/44-hot-cold-or-lukewarm-revelation-315-16/

How to Contact the Author

To learn more about Katie Brazelton, Ph.D., M.Div., M.A., bestselling author, Life Purpose Coach®, and founder of Life Purpose Coaching Centers International® (LPCCI), and her dream of opening 200 Life Purpose Coaching Centers worldwide, contact her at...

Life Purpose Coaching Centers Intl
P.O. Box 80550-0550
Rancho Santa Margarita, CA 92688
Info@LifePurposeCoachingCenters.com
www.LifePurposeCoachingCenters.com

To invite Katie to give a life-changing, keynote speech (with her special touch of humor) to your organization, contact Ambassador Speakers Bureau in Tennessee at (615) 370-4700 or Naomi@AmbassadorSpeakers.com

Katie has been a featured guest for radio and television broadcasts, such as *Midday Connection* and *100 Huntley Street*. She's written more than 60 articles for publications such as *Alive!* and *Extraordinary Women*. She's been honored to meet with Mother Teresa in India and other Nobel laureates around the world. She's been invited to speak at such venues as Focus on the Family and the American Association of Christian Counselors' World Conferences.

Currently, Katie is a professor at Rockbridge Seminary, and she served previously as a licensed minister at the purpose driven Saddleback Church in California. Her coach training organization, LPCCI, which is accredited by the International Coach Federation and the International Association of Continuing Education Training, teaches online and on-site, coed, coach training classes. Katie has two adult children, a daughter-in-law and son-in-law, and two precious grandsons. Check out Katie's other purpose series books, DVD, and CD!

The Way I'm Wired: Discovering Who God Made ME to Be

(DVD Youth Curriculum: UPC 646847-16782-9)
simplyyouthministry.com

How Your Teenager is Wired: Discovering Who God Made Your Teenager to Be

(paperback devotional: ISBN 978-0-764-44705-1)
simplyyouthministry.com

- *Pathway to Purpose for Women* (paperback: ISBN 978-0-310-29249-4)

- *Pathway to Purpose for Women* (audio CD: ISBN 978-0-310-26505-4)

- *Pathway to Purpose for Women* (audio download: ISBN 978-0-310-26857-4)

- *Praying for Purpose for Women* (paperback: ISBN 978-0-310-29284-5)

- *Conversations on Purpose for Women** (spiral-bound: ISBN 978-0-310-25650-2)
  (*A few charts in this book were significantly revised and adapted for use in the Wired series.)

- *Character Makeover* (paperback: ISBN 978-0-310-25653-3)

- *Live Big* (paperback: ISBN 978-1-4391-356-0)